HANDBOOK FOR COACHING CROSS-COUNTRY AND RUNNING EVENTS

George R. Colfer

Parker Publishing Company, Inc. / West Nyack, N.Y

© 1977, *by*

PARKER PUBLISHING COMPANY, INC.

West Nyack, N.Y.

Library of Congress Cataloging in Publication Data

Colfer, George R
    Handbook for coaching cross-country and running
events.

        1. Running. 2. Track-athletics coaching. I. Ti-
tle.
GV1062.C64   796.4'2   76-44356
ISBN 0-13-377051-6

Printed in the United States of America

to the memory of my grandfather

EDWARD PARKER BOYER

How This Book Will Benefit You—The Coach!

The cross-country and track coach of today has to be a master technician. There is no substitute for knowledge and organization in coaching runners. The more knowledge you can acquire on running, the better the performance of your runners is likely to be.

This book gives you detailed information and innovative coaching techniques for a successful running program. It will be of great benefit to those of you who demand complete detail in the organization of your program.

The coaching of cross-country is presented in full detail. Four chapters provide information on such topics as: the different training methods; how to motivate cross-country runners; how to determine the weekly mileage necessary for optimum performance; how to determine when and how to use two-a-day training; putting variety into the training schedule; how to train for different courses, terrains, and distances; peaking for championship meets; how to plan meet strategies; scouting opponents in cross-country; how to utilize cross-country training techniques; plus planning the entire training year including off-season and summer training as well as pre-, early-, mid-, and late-season training schedules.

The chapters on distance and middle-distance events give specific details for screening young runners as well as classifying different types of runners. The Set System of Interval Training as presented here has been cited internationally as a most effective and efficient form of interval training. The Set System is explained thoroughly to improve performance for all levels of runners. The importance of the preliminary distance buildup plus race strategies and tactics are also presented. Some of the other topics covered for the distance and middle-distance events are: how to begin training the unconditioned runner; the use of speed training; and how to adapt to indoor running. Complete training schedules are presented utilizing two unique methods. Included are training cycles for each time of the season, plus an explanation of the different types of training days utilized to help you in planning your specific training needs.

Two chapters cover important techniques for the sprint and hurdle events such as: how to select and classify sprint and hurdle athletes; the importance of distance training for the sprint and hurdle athlete; how to plan and train for more than one event and for trials, finals, and consecutive-day competition; the importance of the sprint and hurdle finish; innovative, yet practical drills for use in these events; and race strategies and tactics. A complete step-by-step analysis of each sprint and hurdle event is presented from start to finish. These analyses give many important tips in order to have your sprint and hurdle athletes run a more efficient and effective race. Training cycles and types of training days are presented for the sprint and hurdle events including off-season or fall training for those runners not participating in cross-country.

The chapter on relays will add a valuable dimension to your relay teams. The real importance of relays to a track team is discussed. "Passing the baton" contains and illustrates the most efficient techniques and tells how you can add "free distance" to all of your passes. The chapter also tells how to select and position runners to improve performance for both the sprint and distance relays. The relays are covered from "start to finish" in all aspects.

A new concept featured is that of "running posture." Some of the topics covered are: how to improve running posture; development of relaxation in running; how to determine if a runner is using mechanics and form to his best advantage; the difference between mechanics and form for sustained running and sprinting; and how to recognize and determine posture-related faults.

A question often asked is "Is strength training necessary for runners?" The answer to this and other questions about strength training appear in chapter 11, "How to Organize and Coach Strength Training for Runners." Specific programs are given for runners of different events and for different times of the season. This chapter also tells how to integrate strength training into the training program without affecting the regular training schedule. Illustrations are included for many important exercises that are beneficial to the runner.

The improvement of running speed is essential to improving the performance of all runners. Running speed can be improved! Speed is analyzed and the areas for speed improvement and the selection of specific programs are thoroughly discussed. Specific programs for the improvement of running speed are given in complete detail to fit the individual needs of any runner. This includes a fully illustrated program on extensive flexibility training.

This book will provide cross-country and track coaches with techniques and innovations that have proved successful in coaching the running game.

——George R. Colfer

ACKNOWLEDGMENTS

I am indebted to numerous individuals who made this book possible.

Gratitude is extended to the athletic department and administrative staff members of St. Bonaventure University, who allowed me the opportunity to coach and develop a Cross-country, Indoor, and Outdoor Track program befitting the University. Specifically: Fr. Canisius F. Connors OFM, Moderator of Athletics; Fr. Cornelius A. Welch OFM, Executive Vice President and Chairman of the Athletic Board; and Mr. Lawrence J. Weise, Director of Athletics.

Special thanks to Mr. John L, Griffith, Publisher of *Athletic Journal*, who provided me with my first opportunity to publish and for permission to use photographs from the *Journal* for the chapter on relays in this book.

I wish to express my appreciation to my wife, Dorothy, who typed the manuscript, and children, Katherine and Edward, for their understanding and patience in this endeavor.

Finally, a special note of thanks to all the high school and college athletes I've had the opportunity to coach in cross-country and track. I sincerely hope that they enjoyed the experiences and memories as much as I have.

Contents

1 How to Organize Cross-Country

Cross-country is unique. It is a sport in which the last man to finish a run is often cheered. It consists mainly of 120 to 150 pounders performing a training schedule that most men could not endure. It is a sport vastly misunderstood by the public. Though cheered in a race, the long distance runner may be subjected to ridicule during his training. The intense training that involves the successful runner is an experience that only those taking part can comprehend. The laymen often ask why. The answer is not precise. Why the runner runs has prompted many answers. The replies **are varied and** this chapter does not intend to dwell on the philosophical. It should suffice to say that the cross-country runner is one of the hardest working athletes in the realm of sport. His reasons are usually his own and more often than not, they only make sense to him.

For the coach, cross-country can be a thoroughly enjoyable experience. The constant challenge and use of strategy in planning the training and competition plus the close association that develops with the runners can provide great personal satisfaction.

PSYCHOLOGICAL PREPARATION FOR CROSS-COUNTRY

The psychological preparation for cross-country consists of one main factor. The runner must prepare himself for pain. He knows that he will encounter pain and that knowledge may bring anxiety. No one likes pain, but it is part of long-distance running. The coach can inform his runners what is going to take place, but only the runner can prepare himself for the task. This involves intense psychological as well as physical preparation on the part of the athlete. To dwell on pain can be unnerving, but must be done in order to displace it by the intrinsic goals of the runner. Running is a total experience. The fulfillment of the run must make the pain worth bearing. The runner almost daily encounters pain and must strive to overcome it. One reason long-distance running becomes such a satisfying experience is that man surpasses himself each time he is able to defeat the pain encounter.

Run for Fun

The concept of "run for fun" is not new, but it is being more openly discussed. No longer is running a form of self-punishment. This is not a contradiction of the previous passage on pain. The enjoyment of running is an extension of the question: Why do men run? It is primarily an individual matter. Enjoyment first comes from possessing a high state of fitness. As fitness improves, the run becomes more efficient and pleasurable. Running can be aesthetic as well as competitive. Some runners find most enjoyment in competing, winning, defeating an opponent, breaking records and the success that follows. Others take their primary pleasure from fitness, being part of a team, independence, solitude, personal achievement, and the exhilaration of hard work. Since most sport is highly structured in its play, these intangible benefits in a sport as individual as cross-country are highly sought. This is not to say that the more aesthetic runner is not a competitor. The athlete who achieves great personal satisfaction from running is more than likely to be a strong competitor because he does enjoy himself!

The coach can add to these satisfactions by creating a training atmosphere that is free from excessive regimentation and pressure. The training sessions should be enjoyable and not a burden. The dedicated runner is going to be willing to work hard. Each practice session should not be made into a stressful situation. Even the ones that need to be should be approached calmly and the objectives stated. Training is preparation for competition, not competition itself. Success can take many forms in long-distance running: a team victory, an individual win, a place, a personal best in time, a spirited kick to the finish in defeating an opponent. These are a few of the successes in competition. However, the coach whose only message in long-distance running is "Win," may find the interests of his runners much different from his.

A Distinct Competitive Season

There is no doubt that fall cross-country is going to improve the spring track performances of the distance runners as well as those of other runners. However, cross-country is a distinct and separate sport in its own right. It is not just preliminary training for track. There are many runners who prefer cross-country competition to track. The freedom that is offered to the athlete in this sport is rare in the world of structured athletics. Cross-country should be coached, organized, and administrated with consideration and enthusiasm equal to that for any other sport in the athletic program.

THE CROSS-COUNTRY ATHLETE

Cross-country is for the runner with desire. He must want to excel in his sport. Body types and size do offer some physical limitations. The ideal cross-country runner is lean and muscular in build, weighs about 120 to 150 pounds at a height of 5'6" to 6'0". While height is more variable, I have never known of an outstanding competitive 200 pound cross-country runner. The largest athlete I coached in cross-country was 6'3" and 170 pounds. An outstanding middle-distance runner in track, he was either our number one, two, or three man in cross-country over a three year period as well as a team captain.

Cross-Country for Whom?

The appeal of cross-country is mainly to those athletes interested in long and middle-distance running. However, there has been a myth that sprinters should not run cross-country. I believe this is false and have encouraged runners of all events to compete in cross-country. For their final three years, two of my top sprinters participated wholeheartedly in cross-country. There were no ill effects from the distance training. In fact, one of these runners actually found himself to be a better quarter-miler as a result of the distance work whereas before he mainly ran the 100 and 200. In his third year of cross-country, this sprinter elevated himself to the number 5 position and was elected team captain. I would like to emphasize that these runners were not forced into cross-country, but participated by their own choice.

As a general rule, all runners of track should be encouraged to participate in cross-country. If they choose to participate, they should actively train and compete for a position on the team. Off-season distance training may be handled separately.

To be a highly motivated cross-country runner, one must disassociate all thoughts of track preparation. The mind must concentrate on what is happening now and not project ahead. One of the greatest excuses for poor performance in cross-country is "I'm only out to get in shape for track." If this is what the runner believes, this is what he will produce. He will not approach the quality of performance that he would if he would place all the emphasis on cross-country. Many successful cross-country runners are successful track runners, but this does not always work in reverse. For the track athlete who is not able to concentrate fully on cross-country, the off-season distance buildup for track will be just as effective. He can train on a strictly non-competitive basis outside of the cross-country team influence.

Motivation of Runners

Cross-country runners are basically self-motivated athletes. In other words, those that want it will go get it. The exception may be the novice runner for whom all aspects of the sport are new. The guidance and supervision of the coach may help the novice through these early stages and build his confidence and knowledge. If the new runner is definitely motivated, he will steadily develop and become more independent in his motivation.

I recall a young runner whom I began to coach at the age of 14. Almost daily, he would literally collapse after the workouts. After deciding he was in no medical danger, I slowly encouraged him to strive daily to break this habit and accept the pain as part of the sport. Thinking he would soon quit, I admired his determination and kept encouraging him as well as being firm in my approach. Two years later, he was a fine high school distance runner as well as a finalist in the state meet mile run.

While extrinsic rewards do motivate and are important, the cross-country runner must have intrinsic desires and self-motivation to dedicate himself to the run.

Discipline of Runners

Discipline in cross-country is twofold. First of all, the dedicated runner will possess a large amount of self-discipline. There is no other route to success. The athlete who does not have self-discipline and who does not respond to any form of motivation will probably hang it up. However, in any group of young, healthy athletes, firmness in handling is needed. The coach can avoid many discipline problems by being well organized, consistent, and knowledgeable in his approach to cross-country. Even the finest athlete at one time or another may require some sort of discipline. The following guidelines are suggested to maintain the best possible discipline for a cross-country team.

1. Display a positive approach to the sport.
2. Be well planned and organized.
3. Use encouragement whenever possible instead of negativism.
4. Display fairness and equality to all.
5. Be consistent in the handling of the athletes.
6. Do not make rules or regulations that you will not or cannot enforce.
7. Use a firm approach when and if problems do arise; however, show flexibility when the situation demands.
8. Make the most use of the coach-captain and captain-team relationship.
9. Offer the athletes some opportunities to participate in the planning of any team rules or regulations.

ORGANIZING THE CROSS-COUNTRY PROGRAM

Competitive Distances

At the interscholastic level, most competitive distances are run from between two and three miles with about two and one half miles being the most common distance. On the intercollegiate level, the races can be from three to seven miles, with the average about five miles.

Since college freshmen are now eligible for varsity competition, it would seem reasonable to have the high schools increase their competitive distances to about four miles. Most high school runners have not yet quite developed the love of the distance run that the seasoned college runner feels. Therefore, the increase of the race distance would enable them to adjust more easily to the college distances and also give them a more realistic view of cross-country. Since most high school coaches use training methods comparable to that of the colleges, there is little reason why the distances could not be increased. It would prove beneficial to the athletes planning to participate in future cross-country and would not cause any health or physical problems since the training distances well surpass the race distances.

By using longer distances the transition from high school to college or independent road running would be less difficult, and the variables which make cross-country so great a sport would be even more present.

Designing the Course

The initial factor in designing the course is the distance desired and the area available. The course should be designed to provide variation and a challenging run. While the home course advantage can be of some importance, one must also prepare to run away meets. Therefore, the design should provide the types of terrain that will be encountered on away trips.

The location of your school and the area or facilities available obviously influence the course design, but by using all available resources such as golf courses, city or state parks, etc., one can usually design a challenging and appealing course.

Another idea is to use variable course distances throughout the season. That is, to start the early season meets with shorter runs and add legs or loops to the course increasing the distance of the runs as the season matures and builds towards the championship meets. Having a longer course may give a definite home advantage over the schools that have shorter courses, especially early in the season.

Some guidelines for designing or re-designing your cross-country course are as follows.

1. Make the course as non-repetitious as possible. The most boring runs are those that constantly circle or otherwise repeat themselves.
2. Add as much variety to the terrain as possible. Include hills, valleys, grass, trails, woods, etc.
3. Avoid crowded roads or excessive use of highways. The traffic may provide a hazard or cause a tragedy.
4. Avoid any questionable turns or cut offs which may confuse the runners or actually cheat the away team.
5. Have the course permanently marked. Paint or markers placed on trees, landmarks, etc. will supplement the flags and required markers especially as these are sometimes misplaced or taken.
6. If possible, design the route of the course so that there will be areas for spectators to gather and watch the run.
7. Have the finish area and chute clearly marked and of permanent quality. If possible, allow about a quarter mile of flat terrain in which to allow the runner to assess his sprint to the finish line.
8. At the chute or finish line, have some available facility in which

spectators can gather. This may be as simple as a hillside, a bleacher, or an accessible school area.

In summary, the cross-country course should be interesting, challenging, provide variation in terrain, be safe, provide spectator accessibility, be clearly marked and not confusing for any opponent.

Number of Races per Season

There are two approaches to take in planning the number of competitive races during the season. Each approach is based on a coaching philosophy and the season's purpose or goal. The number of races does not necessarily have to correspond to the team's win and loss record as most schools now run multiple dual meets during one race.

The first approach which is probably most popular today is that of competing once weekly and then having five to six training days. The advocates of this approach definitely intend to improve their performance through the weekly training sessions and are pointing for the late season championship meets. This is not to say that they do not intend to win on the way to the top, but that the full training week is a necessity and that one competitive run is enough. Usually this competition is with more than one team, possibly up to three or four, and is usually on a Friday or Saturday. The weekly competition is a planned indicator of the week's progress. The coaches using this approach to competition usually run between eight and ten meets during the season.

The second approach is one of improving performance through the use of competition. This means running competitive races twice weekly or three times in two weeks. Once the athletes are in good condition, it is felt that the training will not produce the same increase in performance as will the extra competition. The advocates of this method will not run the same mileage as those using the first approach, but feel that the quantity of competition will make up the difference. The number of races with this method usually will be from twelve to fourteen for the season. One point to mention is that the heaviest concentration of meets is in midseason and even the most enthusiastic coaches using this method will taper off the two a week competition prior to the late season or championship meets. The main point to watch with this approach is that the runner does not weary of competition too early in the season; whereas the advocates of one race per week must work to maintain the interests of their runners throughout the training week.

While both approaches to competition have merit and can be justified, the trend seems to be that the more experienced or higher caliber runner will benefit more from the one a week competition, while the novice or untested runner may improve more rapidly through the use of more competition.

Most coaches have probably experimented or used both methods depending upon their material and have found what appears to work best with the athletes and program at their disposal.

A suggested sample of a cross-country schedule which would prove challenging and interesting for the season is as follows. The exact dates would vary with different years and the different conferences, states, or areas of the country.

OFF-SEASON PRACTICE—Summer schedule through the mail.
PRESEASON PRACTICE—Begin on Monday, August 27 with two a day sessions.
CLASSES BEGIN—September 4—One a day formal workouts. Morning workout on own.
(Wednesday) September 12—Relay Meet—Home—Five to seven schools invited, four men to a team, each school can enter as many teams as desired. Team trophies and individual awards given. Each runner runs a two mile leg.
(Saturday) September 22—Triangular Meet—Home.
(Saturday) September 29—Triangular Meet—Away.
(Wednesday) October 3—Dual Meet—Home.
(Saturday) October 6—Triangular Meet—Away.
(Saturday) October 13—Quadrangular Meet—Home.
(Tuesday) October 16—Triangular Meet—Away.
(Saturday) October 20—Triangular Meet—Home.
(Saturday) October 27—Invitational Meet—Away.
(Saturday) November 3—Conference Championship Meet—Away.
(Saturday) November 10—Regional Championship Meet—Away.
(Saturday) November 17—State Championship Meet—Away.

How Much Distance?

The most controversial subject in cross-country training is how much total distance should be run each training week. There are many factors that contribute to the mileage a runner needs to be successful. The following must be considered in assessing a runner's total mileage.

1. What experience and background does the runner possess?
2. What is the competitive distance being trained for?
3. Is the runner working out once or twice per day?
4. How many days are included in the training week?
5. How many competitive races are to be run?

6.   What type of training is being included in the schedule: that is quality (interval, speed, pace, etc.) versus quantity?

Other variables such as weather, studies, and personal obligations all can cause fluctuations in the weekly mileage total. Also, the time of the season plays an important role.

The amount of mileage needed for top performance may vary with the individual runner. It depends on the type of runner he is and what his needs are. Many coaches and runners think that the more mileage covered the better, but often this is not the case. Many great runners do attempt and complete 100 to 120 mile training weeks while still in school. However, not all athletes need or can expect to achieve this total in their schedule. We are all familiar I am sure with the tremendous performances of Ben Jipcho, who trains on 40 mile weeks and plenty of rest. It is easy to say "All my athletes run 100 mile training weeks." The question is, is it necessary? The total mileage covered should bring the runner to his optimum potential, but should not overtire him.

The following chart (Table 1-1) suggests the mileage which is practical for the type of program being used so that the athlete can be successful in his endeavors.

Two-a-Day Training

Two-a-day training is practiced by most successful and experienced runners. If most coaches and runners had their own way, they would use double workouts. It is almost impossible to attain the higher mileage rates desired by only one session per day. A quick review of Table 1-1 should make this point clear. However, if two-a-day workouts are to be used, they should be done methodically and for a purpose. All runners are not ready for this experience, especially on the interscholastic level. Some athletes, especially younger ones, may not possess sufficient strength to endure double workouts. Also, if the training proves too intense, the runner may lose interest. When we talk of the two-a-day, 120 mile workout week of a great college runner, it can hardly be compared to the week of the average high school runner. Most cross-country teams at the high school level have runners with a much wider range of ability and interest than that of the national class runner. It is most important to design workouts to fit the individual needs of a runner. This is where the morning workout can prove a bonus to the runner who needs and wants the extra work.

The primary purposes for the morning workout are as follows:

1.   To attain the desired mileage in the training week.

TABLE 1-1
TOTAL WEEKLY MILEAGE

TYPE OF PROGRAM			TIME OF SEASON			
DAILY WORKOUTS	TRAINING DAYS	WEEKLY COMPETITION	PRE SEASON	EARLY	MID	LATE
2	7	1	84	75	70	65
2	7	more than 1	84	71	66	61
2	6	1	78	69	64	59
2	6	more than 1	78	65	60	55
1	7	1	70	62	58	54
1	7	more than 1	70	58	54	50
1	6	1	60	52	48	44
1	6	more than 1	60	48	44	40

NOTE: This mileage table is designed for the experienced high school runner who has used a summer training program to prepare for the season. The distances would need modification for the novice or beginning runner as well as those who have not engaged in summer training.

2. To loosen up for the afternoon session.
3. To cover longer distances to build endurance and strength.

It is important however that the morning workout does NOT:

1. Impair the performance and effectiveness of the afternoon workout.
2. Overtire the athlete so that he cannot train at his best.
3. Cause the athlete to lose interest in running.
4. Become a stressful situation.

The majority of morning workouts are not supervised by the coach. The time of the run is usually left up to the athlete as long as it is completed at least four hours prior to the afternoon session, and a set weekly mileage total is accomplished. By letting the runner choose his workout site and time, you are allowing him to enjoy the freedom of cross-country even though he may have a highly regimented afternoon workout.

The majority of morning workouts are strictly distance runs at a relaxed pace. Above all, they should be enjoyable and not produce fatigue. I have come across many fine athletes who as college freshmen were completely burned out and lost interest in running as a result of highly stressful and regimented high school careers.

The type of morning workout can vary, but nine out of ten coaches I have known use this time strictly for distance. The generally agreed upon AM workout would be as follows: Three or four days per week depending upon the competitive schedule, take a distance run of from three to five miles. Aim for a weekly morning total of twelve to twenty miles.

Another type of AM workout some coaches have found successful is to first loosen up with a one to two mile run, then run 110 yard acceleration strides with a 30 second pause between runs, finishing off with another one to two mile run.

The best way to determine the need and the use of the morning workout is to suit it to the individual athlete. The AM workout will vary according to his level and needs. As stated previously, it is no secret that our country's great runners all use two-a-day training. However, be sure the athlete is ready for it and that it will be helpful to him and not harmful. If an athlete shows signs of overtiring during his afternoon training and in competition, possibly a lightening of his morning schedule would remedy this situation.

The morning workouts are described in chapter 4, "The Cross-Country Training Program," for the different times of the season and in conjunction with the competitive schedule.

Where to Train

The training for cross-country can take place almost anywhere. However the more training sites available, the more will be the appeal of the program. By using all facilities within the reach of his team, the coach will be less likely to lose the interest of his runners and should be well prepared for any course his team may encounter. The home course should be utilized, but not as the only training site, although certain parts of the course may do well for interval work, speed training, etc. The use of different training sites depends much upon where you are located.

Some suggestions for use as different training sites are as follows:

1. City or town parks	10. Beaches
2. State parks	11. Lakesides
3. Country clubs or golf courses	12. Hill trails
4. Roads (stress safety)	13. Ski trails
5. Campus roads and walks	14. Hiking trails
6. Athletic fields	15. Farm roads
7. The track	16. Pipeline or dike trails
8. Open grassy areas	17. Power line trails
9. Woods or forests	

The distance and mileage of all training sites should be known and accurate. The coach should also check yearly to make sure the same sites are still runnable and accessible to his team.

Variety in Training

Variety in training is most essential to the mental and physical well being of the runner. Too much repetition can become dangerous in training as the athletes' interest and performance may decrease. There are two common ways in which to provide variety in training. The first was discussed in the previous section, that is to change the training site as often as feasible. The second way is to provide variety in the type of workouts being performed. This method pertains mainly to the afternoon workout. Often the weekly workout schedule is not too different from that of the previous week. By the use of variety in the format, staleness should not occur. The simplest method of doing this is to alternate a long distance day and a day of interval, speed, etc. However, providing variety is a bit more challenging than this alone. Suggestions for providing variety in the workouts are:

1. Make use of different training sites.
2. Use different distances.
3. Run in different groups or change partners.
4. Use changes of pace.
5. Set different objectives for different days.
6. On occasion, run the courses or trails in reverse.
7. Vary interval workouts and interval recoveries.
8. Vary the requirements for Fartlek runs.

9.   Have special workouts for special situations.
10.   Try to add something different to each day's practice.

The Use of the Track

For some cross-country runners, the track is known as the "nightmare." However, the track can have a purpose in cross-country. It is a place to check out pace and time for shorter distances or intervals. The use of the track should not be excessive. Most work on the track can be done in other areas without the monotony. The coach who depends mostly on the track for his cross-country workouts may be missing the point of the sport and is not offering enough variety to his runners. As a general rule the track should not be included in the weekly training schedule more than once.

Preparation of Workouts

It would take years of experience in the same coaching situation with the same runners to set up a yearly workout plan that is foolproof. Therefore, it is impractical to try to set up a season piece by piece before it occurs. A suggested way to prepare workouts is given in the following format.

1.   Decide on a flexible general plan of the season based on the schedule, starting date, number of training days, and the abilities of the returning athletes.
2.   Lay out a block plan for each of the four phases of the season (Pre—Early—Mid—Late).
3.   Make up a detailed weekly plan for the coming training week at the completion of the prior week.
4.   Review the practice plan on the day of the practice. Another way is to sit down immediately after a practice and review the next day's plan.
5.   If a plan needs changing, do it prior to the practice session.
6.   Take into account the conditions of the day and of the athletes and be flexible.

Other methods involve having the athletes help in the daily planning or having more than one workout prepared for each session. Flexibility and readiness to adjustment are marks of the successful experienced coach.

Flexibility in Training Schedules

Flexibility in the training schedule is a must. However, this flexibility works in both directions. If the responses of the athletes indicate change, and they are overtired, not tired enough, lacking challenge, or bored, then the coach should be able to change the remainder of the workout. These changes do not mean discarding the workout, but consist mainly of changing distances, paces, intervals, sprints, and number of repetitions, or of using substitutions such as changing hill work to 110 acceleration strides. Any change should be meaningful and have a purpose.

The weather can also influence a change in the workout. Extremes of cold, heat, humidity, and rain or snow are reasons for flexibility. However, since most cross country meets go in all conditions, one must not use these as an excuse for not training.

The use of flexibility in the case of a single runner can present a problem. While the trainer knows best how hard an injured athlete can work, the coach must exercise judgment in handling injury and other situations. There is no set rule or answer to this problem. You must know your athletes!

Supervision of Workouts

I firmly believe that the coach should supervise the cross-country workout. This may exclude the morning runs, but does not mean the coach must stay away. It would depend upon how he preset the training and his availibility.

Whether the coach supervises by foot, by car, by bicycle, or by golf cart, he should be in charge of the practice. The session should be started by the coach and he should be present at the completion of the training. I have found this to be a very satisfactory time to really get to know the runners. On long distance runs, unless they are timed and check points are important, the coach does not always need to be beside the runners, but he should be present as they return and stay until the last man is in. During interval work, he should be present to supervise and in some cases motivate the athletes.

I use running or jogging as a technique for my own fitness. I do not expect to run the same times as the younger athletes, but my runners do know I can run and on occasion will go with them. A method I found quite beneficial to both of us was to jog the warm up, usually one to two miles to the training site for the day. Then we would proceed with the day's training which of course I did not participate in except as a coach. Then I would join them for the same run back. We would stay as a group and enjoy lots of conversation on the way. For long distance runs, especially those well away from campus, I found the use of a car at two mile checkpoints effective. On occasion where the runners did not all cover the same areas, I would set myself up at a standard checkpoint where the runners knew they would find me. I do not feel it is necessary or practical for all coaches to run with their athletes, but it offers one way to participate in the training session and have interaction with your runners. Two extreme examples come to my mind: One was a coach I ran under who would pace our intervals in track on a bicycle. We seemed always to tire before he did! The other was a cross-country coach who never supervised his runners' workouts. He just posted them on the locker room board. Before one meet, he was unable to recall the names of his runners to be entered in the race. I often wondered how much this impersonal attitude impaired the performance of his runners.

Motivational Devices

While I previously stated that most successful cross-country runners are self-motivated and although many people today think of the modern athlete as too sophisticated to fall for cliches, the cross-country runner looks to more than self-motivation for his success in running. Most coaches use some motivational devices. All of these devices are not just rewarding in nature, but informative as well. Many will lead the runner towards his own self-motivation and aid him when he faces hard times in the sport. Also, many of these devices tend to promote team unity and the idea that for a team to be successful, the individual must become part of the team.

The following are devices that I have used or obtained from other successful coaching colleagues.

1. Pride in individual effort.
2. Pride in team effort.
3. Building or continuing traditions.
4. Competing to make varsity team or traveling squad.
5. Election of team captain.
6. Publicity in school newspaper.
7. Publicity in local newspapers.

8. Mileage awards (off season and in season).
9. Letter awards.
10. Season awards (Best—Most Improved—MVP—etc.).
11. MVP per meet.
12. Summer letters from coach.
13. Captain's letter before first meet.
14. Team get togethers (usually during preseason or on a Sunday —picnics, outings with a run included).
15. Unannounced or surprise contests in which shirts, shorts, jox or sox may be given as rewards. These are used for practices, not meets.
16. Scouting Board—the posting of the opponent's results and times.
17. Improvement charts.
18. Posting of meet and season times.
19. Results of meets printed up for handouts.
20. Preseason brochures.
21. Post season summaries.
22. Team and individual pictures.
23. Publicize meets to attract spectators.
24. Home course records.
25. Best course performances—opponents included, top 50 times.
26. Best course performances—home team only, top 25 times.
27. Time clubs or awards, etc., for breaking a challenging time on the home course.
28. Slogans, sayings, poems, etc., if applicable and appropriate to cross-country.
29. THE PERSONAL INTEREST OF THE COACH IN HIS ATH-LETES.

The Coach's Role

To summarize the role of the coach in the organization of cross-country is to state that he must first be knowledgeable of the sport and then be an organizer, a planner, and an administrator. He then can further enhance his role by showing a sincere personal interest in his athletes. Experience in the coach can only come from time and knowledge. However, enthusiasm and effort come from within and can begin the first day a man becomes a coach.

2 *Methods and Techniques for Cross-Country*

THE DIFFERENT TRAINING METHODS

In the last seventy years or so, there have been numerous attempts to define one training method that would be best for all distance runners. That one has never materialized. Usually a new method becomes popular due to the success of world class runners who train with that method. However, this does not mean that it will be successful for all who undertake it. Most methods used by the experienced world class runners do not fit the needs or programming of the scholastic runner. Therefore the ideas in articles or textbooks have to be adapted to the program. In theory we may advocate one such method, but the actual training may not be the same. An excellent example of this is in Lydiard's Marathon method. He states 100 miles per week is essential, therefore a 100 mile week following marathon training principles would seem to fulfill this method. However, Lydiard has stated that while Snell and other of his greats did cover 100 miles in regular training, their warm-up and cooling down periods plus other jogging sometimes resulted in 200 to 250 mile weeks. This would be hard to accomplish on the scholastic level.

There follows a brief description of the five most prominent training methods for distance running. Very few coaches use one method alone, but combine the various methods into techniques for use in their programs. No one method is advocated or rejected.

Fartlek

This method which means "Speed Play" is of Swedish origin. Gunder Haegg was the originator of the system, while Gosta Holmer of

Sweden, a former national coach, popularized and described the system. It consists of long-distance runs for time or mileage involving the use of different terrains, locations, and mainly different rates of speed ranging from a full sprint to a slow jog. The different variables and combinations are meant to provide an invigorating and stimulating form of training without inducing complete fatigue or at least an awareness of fatigue. Fartlek should be done in pleasant, relaxing surroundings, aesthetic to the runner and possessing terrain variety. It should create an enjoyable experience. However Fartlek training must be organized and purposeful. The training performed correctly is most demanding and can prove very effective. Percy Cerutty's tactics in long-distance training approached the Fartlek method, but with much more intensity than most coaches would deem necessary. Fartlek corresponds to natural running and although by no means new, it is still used extensively in long-distance training.

LSD (Long Slow Distance)

This method advocates that through the use of slower and longer runs, the athlete will build himself up to performances that he could not attain otherwise. It states that speed training is very overrated in distance running. LSD promotes fun or enjoyment in running. Its philosophy is to train slower and race faster, and enjoy the experience while doing it. They call it "the love of the run." Arthur Newton is attributed to be the founder of LSD well over fifty years ago, while Joe Henderson has done much for its modern adaptation. The modern LSD concept came into existence in the mid-sixties. Basically its trainees use no speed training. They depend on the race itself for that. LSD has been used by many top runners, especially marathoners. It is also widely used in the recuperation of overtired or disinterested runners.

Interval

Interval training is a period of work or exercise followed by a measured recovery. It is a form of regimented Fartlek; that is, fast and slow running. It features a measured run with a measured recovery. There are many ways that interval training may be planned and used. The method itself is generally attributed to Franz Stampfl and the training system of Emil Zatopek. Many of the great distance runners of the fifties and early sixties were intensely trained by the interval method.

Interval training is much maligned and much used. Very few

coaches would use interval training as an only method, but it does have a place in all types of distance running when properly used. Interval training is thoroughly discussed in a later chapter.

Marathon

This method was designed and developed by Arthur Lydiard and is widely accepted in the coaching field. The marathon training bases its success on seven days a week, two-a-day training, averaging 100 miles per week and training for 52 weeks per year. The degree of intensity varies with the season or the time of the year. This is for the mature runner. Most races are part of the training as intense preparation is given to only a few races per year. Lydiard also states that speed requires specific sprint training. One reason the marathon system has caught on is that the program offers a good training balance for both cross-country and track. The Lydiard method is broken into stages, each progressing as the runner is ready. As an example, distance running is stressed completely until the runner is proven ready to advance to interval, speed, or hill training. The marathon training is based on the entire year and each stage or phase is planned accordingly. While the strong point of the marathon system is a gradual buildup of stamina and strength, a weakness of the school programs is that they are more seasonal and may consist of different attitudes towards competition, especially that of team competition. The completely undiluted Lydiard marathon program may be too extreme for the scholastic athlete, although it has been much proven in world class runners. Lydiard's success is due to careful, detailed planning for his runners as well as the use of sound physiological principles. Marathon training is a patient method featuring a "train, don't strain" attitude. Those that would overintensify or rush Lydiard's training would not be accomplishing the full value of it.

Tempo

Tempo training in long-distance running is a method by which all training is to be done at or near race pace. It means full effort into all training. In other words, slow running is a waste of time; for example, if you are going to run for one hour, run as fast as possible for that entire length of time. Interval work is also included in tempo training, but with non-stop recovery intervals, and the run interval is again done at full effort. One must be a very strong individual to withstand a full season of this training. The total mileage would not be as high as for that of other methods. A noted distance runner, Derek Clayton, although professing no one method, trains by the tempo philosophy; that is performing all of his training at full effort. Tempo training has resulted in sensational times for some runners, while for others it has led to injury or discouragement. High tempo training submits to the P.T.A. philosophy (P.T.A. stands for pain, torture, agony), which means that unless the training hurts, it does no good in improving the runner.

THE TECHNIQUES OF CROSS-COUNTRY TRAINING

The Warm-up

A period of warm-up is essential in cross-country. Some may argue this point, and while research has shown findings favoring both pro and con, one must be conscious of the needs of the individual runner. The best warm-up for running is running. The actual warm-up will depend upon the type of workout to be performed. At the very beginning of a season, a team warm-up is a boost for team morale and also teaches the runners what loosening up routines and exercises to use. After that period, the warm-up is handled in one of three ways.

1. *Formal Warm-up*—This is led by the coach and/or captain and consists of calisthenics, jogging, and possibly some drills prior to the daily workout.
2. *Individual Warm-up*—The runners are instructed to be warmed up and ready to go when the practice time arrives. Time may be allotted for this by putting this time into the training schedule or the runner must get himself out early enough to sufficiently warm up. This works well for experienced runners, but the novice runner must receive some prior instruction.
3. *Automatic Warm-up*—Part of the workout itself is scheduled as a warm-up. Example: A two mile run to the training site will serve as the warm-up. Once there, five to ten minutes is given to the athletes to prepare for the coming workout on their own. Incidentally, the warm-up that the athlete finds most beneficial to his practice performance is the same warm-up he should use before a race. This will enable him to be physically prepared as well as psychologically content that he is ready to run.

LSD

Long Slow Distance is one way of accomplishing some of the mileage needed in cross-country. As part of the program and not an entire method by itself, it may be incorporated into the training schedule at any time. LSD is used in our training system for runs of five to fifteen miles at a comfortable pace in which the runner is not over-fatigued at its completion. LSD is also effective for the morning workouts.

Timed Distance

This is another form of long-distance running for mileage as well as strength and stamina. The difference between LSD and timed distance is that a time limit for the run is set regardless of how much mileage is covered. The time is usually between 30 and 90 minutes. Otherwise, all of the characteristics of LSD apply. Timed distance can produce a relaxing effect in the runner as he knows that regardless of the mileage he puts in, he must run for the entire time limit. This tends to help the runner not to rush his workout.

Fartlek

As previously defined, Fartlek means "speed play." Fartlek runs in cross-country are best used off the track completely and in a natural setting. The Fartlek run if done properly is best kept to a distance of five to six miles. This *may* or *may not* include a warm-up and cooling down period of jogging. Timed Fartlek should not exceed sixty minutes in length and includes the warm-up and cooling down period.

The Fartlek workout can be planned in two ways. The coach can state the distance or time to be covered and the ingredients or requirements of the run. Example: A sixty minute timed run with a:

1. Two-mile warm-up run.
2. 4 x 440 at race pace.
3. 4 x a 50 yard hill (uphill and downhill).
4. 4 x 110 yard acceleration stride.
5. 4 x 50 yard sprint.

Between each of the stated runs, the runner jogs or runs at different paces until he is ready to undertake his next run. The runs do not have to be in order or in sequence, just be completed within the time limit. Any time left is used for distance. The total distance from a workout as described above could be from seven to eight miles depending upon the condition of the athlete. It is suggested that the runner does not walk during cross country Fartlek training, which is stated in some programs. The continuity of the run as well as the changes of pace are most important. In fact, the use of pace change should be encouraged during the recovery and distance part of Fartlek.

The second way of planning Fartlek runs is to state the time or distance to be covered and then let the athlete add the ingredients to the run. This works well with the experienced runner, but not as well with the novice. The training site used will influence the runner's choice of speed play.

Fartlek is an excellent method of combining distance work with a combination of pace and speed work. Fartlek runs allow much freedom and are therefore usually popular with the athletes as well as beneficial to cross-country training. The combinations for Fartlek are endless in variety, length, and intensity, therefore making their incorporation into the training schedule most flexible.

Pace Work

This is based on the method of tempo training as it is the long distance run at a pace comparable or near to that of the runner's race pace. Usually the distance involved here is not more than six miles and a suggested rule to follow is to make the maximum pace run twice the distance of the home course. This type of workout should be used sparingly and early in the training week as the runner will probably feel slightly tired in the next day's training. The distance pace work can also be handled by time instead of mileage. The use of this training may be on the course or at other training sites.

Interval Training

The use of interval training in cross-country may be put into the training schedule once or twice weekly depending on the competition and the time of the season. The more intense work again should be done earlier in the week or at least two full days before competition. The distances for use in cross-country may differ from that of the track.

In cross-country the interval distance used as a minimum should not be less than 220 yards and no more than one mile. Anything less than a 220 would be assessed as speed work even if run by the interval principles. The 440 and 880 are probably the most common distances used in cross country.

Intervals in cross-country are not necessarily administrated under the same principles as in track. Two suggested techniques for the administration of cross-country interval training are:

A.   Set a time limit for the entire run and recovery. Example: 5 minutes is allowed for an 880 interval. The athlete runs the distance in 2:20 and then has 2:40 left for the recovery before the next run.

B.   Run in groups—one group's run is another group's recovery interval.

Interval training does not have to be done on the track; in fact, again, the use of different training sites to perform the interval work is best. In a survey of successful cross-country coaches, interval training ranked second to distance running as the technique the coaches used most in training their runners.

Speed Training

While many advocates of distance running do not rely on any form of speed training, the effective use of short speed distances can be beneficial to many runners. Speed training may be more beneficial to the high school runner, since the distances are shorter and a faster rate of speed is needed. Speed training distances can vary from 50 to 120 yards. 110's are a popular distance for this purpose. The speed work is usually done near or at the end of the workout and can be handled in different ways. Some of these techniques are as follows: (110 yards will be used as the distance for these examples)

1.   Sprint 110, walk or jog slowly 110 to recuperate. Repeat as many times as desired.

2.   Sprint 110, jog slowly 55 yards (½ the sprint distance), walk 55 yards to recuperate. Repeat as many times as desired.

3.   Sprint 110. Rest 30 seconds between each sprint. Repeat as many times as desired.

4.   Break the runners up into groups of four (two at each end of the sprint). Use a shuttle relay system with one runner going at a time. Repeat until the desired number of repetitions is complete.

5.   Give the runners the number of 110's to do and let them complete them individually at their own rate.

6.   Run the 110's in pairs. This stimulates effort especially if the runners are paired by like abilities.

While the shorter sprint distances (50-80 yards) should be run at full effort, the acceleration type of sprint may be more beneficial at 100 to 120 yards.

Terrain Running

This consists of mainly uphill and downhill running. Slopes, grades, trail running and rough terrain should also be considered. Uphill running is practiced and emphasized by most coaches, however a few words about downhill running may be necessary. Many times the runner reaches a peak or crest of a hill and goes down without any regard for form or mechanics. The downhill run should not be characterized by overstriding or poor posture. The runner should be relaxed and not lose control. The keys to downhill running are to land heel first, not overstride, and, if a speed increase is desired, to increase the forward body lean and lower the arms slightly. Above all, the runner must come off the downhill run in complete control of his body.

Running uphill depends mainly upon leg strength, conditioning, and knee lift. The runner should be in fairly good condition before intense hill training is attempted. Otherwise, fatigue may hamper his posture and effectiveness on the hill. A good hill runner may pick up valuable ground against those runners who are not.

Once conditioned and trained for the hills, their use in training should not be overdone. Too much hill work can physically fatigue a runner since there probably is no harder phase of work in cross-country. In the preseason and early season, more hill work can be taken, but this should be tapered off as mid season approaches. Specific hill work performed once weekly at this time should be sufficient. It is also best done early in the week. However the normal use of hill running in LSD, timed distance, etc. should not be harmful as long as it is not excessive.

Some suggestions to incorporate hill running into the workouts are as follows.

1. Run the hills in pairs. This stimulates effort.
2. If possible, circuit the hill. Run up, run down, and jog around to the upward base. Repeat as many times as desired.
3. Incorporate the hills into Fartlek giving the specific number of repetitions to be used.
4. Use hills of different inclines and grades. Be prepared for any situation that one may encounter.
5. Hill running is best done without rest or stopping. Use jogging for recovery.

6. Practice coming off the crest of a hill and maintaining the race pace. It is essential not to slow the pace. If possible in practice, come off the hill and go at race pace for about 60 yards before slowing to the practice pace.
7. Hills must be run with determination. The runner must conquer the hill and not vice versa.

During a previous coaching situation, our hill training was accomplished by the use of the hills which were part of our course, a country club hill with a steep incline, and the use of a mountain road called "Humphrey Hill," which was 7½ miles up and down in length. Its longest uphill grade was 2.1 miles and most difficult. Needless to say, we never ran this route more than 2 or 3 times per season and usually in the early season. Another drill worth mentioning involving the use of hills was at the conclusion of practice to run "2 wins and out" on our steep country club hill. All runners would start on my signal, sprint up the hill, run down, and jog around the base to await the next run. The object was to win twice and then drop out. This is highly motivating. A way to give runners of all abilities an equal chance is to break them into ability level groups for the drill. This was not a daily drill!

Cooling Down

The cooling down period will end the running workout. Cooling down depends upon what type of workout has taken place. Many cool downs can be added to the workout automatically, such as a returning jog or run from the training site to the locker room. The cooling down period is most important after any pace, interval, terrain, or speed work. A distance of one to two miles usually will be sufficient. This running should be relaxed and comfortable. The point of this is that the runner may recuperate from fatigue and end the workout pleasantly tired. His body systems and functions nearly return to the pre-exercise state.

Strength Training

In chapter 11, "How to Organize and Coach Strength Training for Runners," complete programs and details are given for the cross-country athlete. Due to the type of training involved, most strength work for cross-country is done on a maintenance basis.

OTHER TRAINING DEVICES

In addition to the techniques and conventional methods of cross-country training, there are some additional training devices that can be used throughout the season, which have proven successful. Some of these devices may only be used once yearly or so, but through their use, they can add challenge, variation, and enjoyment to the program.

Cross-Country Relays

Relays can be used in a practice situation or as an early season meet. We employed the relay meet one year on an inter-squad basis and enjoyed the experience so much that the following year we invited seven other schools to participate in the meet. It proved an instant success. Awards were given to the top three four man teams as well as the top fifteen times. Each school could enter as many four man teams as they desired, thus participation was open to all. The relay distance was eight miles or four two mile legs. This meet was held ten days to two weeks prior to our first regular season competition after about two weeks of formal practice. The shorter distance served as an excellent indicator of how the runner's pace was progressing. Up to this meet, most of our practice sessions stressed distance and endurance training.

Time Trials

The use of time trials on the home course should not be overdone. I have never felt that excessive use of the time trial as a training device was beneficial. Runners who train together know how they will end up when running against their teammates. Record times will not show up in time trials and the main benefit of such a run is to simulate running under competitive conditions. I have employed a time trial each season one week prior to the first regular meet. This would follow our relay meet. The main objectives I hoped to accomplish were to simulate competition at the race distance, use the run as an indicator of individual pace and performance, and if our first meet was on the road, it helped in the selection of a traveling squad. Time trials run during the season usually have little value and often spoil what may otherwise be a good training day.

Handicap Runs

The use of handicaps can prove a stimulating and challenging device for the cross-country runner. The distances run for handicapping can vary. The handicap can also provide a more stimulating means of running a time trial when necessary. The weaker runner feels he has a chance for success and should be highly motivated. The stronger runner has more pressure put upon him to make up the time or distance given away, but this can be beneficial as often in training, he will not have such a challenge. The handicap run should not be less than two miles and has proven successful to a maximum of ten miles. The major weakness in handicap running is the accuracy of the handicap. To have the weaker runners passed too early ruins motivation for all. Therefore care must be taken to plan them accurately, based on the runners' status at the time of the run. I have encountered numerous formulas and methods for handicapping. I feel the best system is to rely on the coach's knowledge of his own runners. My best results came from taking an average of the home course times as the season progressed and base the handicaps on the difference in times. For runs of more or less distance, the handicap time is then scaled up or down. Using this method, I rarely had more than a one minute separation between twelve to sixteen runners at a handicapped distance of four to five miles.

The handicap run can be handled in one of two ways:

1. All runners start at the same point and finish there. The clock is started as the slowest runner begins and then each runner takes off by signal from the coach as the difference in their handicap from the slowest runner arrives. The scratch runner(s) will go when the slowest runner's handicap is up.
    Example: Using five runners with different handicaps.
    A. Runner A with a handicap of 2 minutes starts off.
    B. Runner B with a handicap of 1:30 seconds starts off 30 seconds later.
    C. Runner C with a handicap of 1:20 seconds starts off 40 seconds after Runner A.
    D. Runner D with a handicap of 35 seconds starts off 1:25 seconds after Runner A.
    E. Runner E, the scratch runner, starts off two minutes after Runner A, completing the total handicap time.
    The delayed starting time is then subtracted from the total time for all

but Runner A to obtain the runner's true time. All runners cover the same amount of distance!

2. By breaking the handicap time into distance or yards, each runner will begin at a different starting point according to his handicap. Upon a common starting signal, all runners start together and finish at the scratch or finish line. Two disadvantages to this method are:

    A. All runners do not run the same distance, therefore any timing is not accurate except for the scratch runners.

    B. Unless a track or extremely open area is used, the common starting signal may be a problem for all runners to hear or see. Also pacing off or setting such distances accurately is time consuming. Since the handicaps should change frequently as will the variety of distances for the runs, this may become very complex. One method of handling this is to have each runner measure off his own distance, usually by pace of foot. Again, accuracy may present a problem with this type of measurement.

Marathon Runs

Many coaches will use the marathon run once weekly to build up the runner's total mileage as well as for strength and stamina. A way in which we used a marathon run for motivation and training was at the conclusion of our formal double sessions. On Labor Day or the Sunday before, we would have a single workout which would be a run from the school campus to another city or town. The road measured distance was about 18 miles. We would start the run in mid-morning, about 10 AM. Two to three cars monitored the run at about two to three mile checkpoints. Towels, fluids, and times were provided for those who wanted them along the way. Safety precautions, including the provision of oxygen, were also taken. At the conclusion of the run, times were given and refreshments provided. After cooling down, the runners were transported back to the school. Often interested students volunteered to help, as did some of the runners' parents.

Off-season marathons were left to the discretion of the athlete. A few of my runners would participate in marathons as long as it did not interfere with their indoor track schedule.

Road Runs

As a rule, most coaches do not want or permit their athletes to run outside competition during the season. I agree with this as too much competition may be detrimental to their performance. Any such runs should be checked out first as to eligibility rules and secondly as to their purpose and conditions by the coach. The exception to this may be a locally sponsored run in which the entry of your team would promote public relations with your town or city.

Indian Run

A very simple training device that can be put into any type of group distance running is a technique that we call the "Indian Run." Actually, it is close to a Fartlek-based run.

The runners, numbered anywhere from four to eight based on ability levels, start their distance run in a line. After the first mile which is used as a warm up and to establish a set pace, the last runner in line sprints to the lead, takes over first position, and then returns to the set pace. This process then goes to the next runner, and the next etc. As each runner becomes last in the line, he sprints to get the lead. It is an excellent device for practicing the passing of runners and for changing paces. One point to mention to the runners is that they should not make their sprint for the lead until the previous man has taken the lead and fallen back into the pace. Do not rush the run! With six runners to a group, each runner will get to sprint once in about 600 to 660 yards. An example of an Indian Run is as follows:

1. Total run—six miles.
2. Pace setting—one mile.
3. Indian Run—three miles.
4. Group run—two miles.

Orienteering Runs

This device is a sport in its own right, but can prove a challenging and invigorating form of cross-country distance training. The sport requires a map, compass, terrain, and a runner. For cross-country purposes, we can do away with the compass and a formal map. The coach and managers etc. will have to spend some time in setting up a course for the runners and it would have to be changed for each orienteering run. It is a good way to establish a new training site or route.

The course should be set up in the following manner:

1. The course would need to be marked prior to the training run. Sugges-

tions are signs or manila folders marked or colored to determine direction tacked on to the various points of the course as needed.

2. To make sure the runners follow the course correctly, colored or numbered tags can be strung from trees, markers, etc. Each runner should grab a tag at each checkpoint and carry it to the finish. Be sure there is a sufficient number of tags at each station for every runner to be able to get one.

3. Before the start of the run, post a course map in the locker room and then verbally explain it at the start. Be sure to explain the marking symbols and how many tags are to be picked up.

4. If all of the runners go in one group, it may become follow the leader. Groups of two to four are best and if time permits, even singles. A group of two seems to work best for cross-country. Start each group one minute or so apart or better yet, when the group ahead is out of sight.

5. The times can be reported or not depending upon the situation. However, most athletes like to know how they ran and who did the best.

6. Initiate certain penalties for not finding all the tags such as extra sprints, exercises, etc. They should not be too severe.

7. If the runner completes the course and returns all the tags, he has finished and should not be penalized regardless of his time.

This type of orienteering run is a "fun" workout. It should provide sound distance training depending upon the distance involved. The runner should never stop nor should he need to. This may be something that is used only once or twice per season, but should provide something that the runners look forward to. It could also be an excellent and interesting way to provide that long Saturday or Sunday workout following competition.

3

Strategy and Meet
Preparation for
Cross-Country

Most teams will try to use some form of meet plan or strategy in running competition. Not only can this be beneficial to the team effort, but it may add to the individual runner's motivation to succeed, as he will know his expected objective for that race. Some coaches prefer to have each individual just do his best and not plan any team strategy. While no outstanding runner should ever be held back or hindered by any strategy, usually a combination of individual and group tactics will lead to the best team effort possible.

RACE STRATEGIES

Bunching

This tactic requires that the runners of a team stay in a "bunch" or run fairly close together. One advantage of bunching is that a weaker runner may be helped by running with his teammates. A team with similar ability levels can be very effective using bunch tactics. It is most demoralizing for an opponent to be passed not by one, but by five or six runners at the same time. Bunch tactics are set until a prearranged point or distance to go in the race when each runner will go all out and finish as best he can. The average distance of maintaining the bunch may be from one half to two thirds of the race, depending mainly upon the competition and the position of the bunch. The bunch must be in a challenging position or running out front. Bunching is a poor strategy if the team is not homogeneous in ability. A strong runner with a weaker bunch may be hindered by this tactic.

Grouping

Grouping is basically the same tactic as bunching, except that in grouping the runners are put into a group by ability levels. Usually in a race two groups are formed and each will run together until the pre-arranged point at which to break for the finish. An advantage of grouping is that no runner is hindered by a slower teammate, nor is a bunch broken up because a weaker runner cannot keep up the pace. The main weakness of grouping is that the second group may not be in contention to finish high enough to win the meet.

Matching Up

This tactic is based on scouting or prior knowledge of the opponents' times and abilities. In matching up, the coach will assign each runner an opponent to run against. The purpose is to defeat that opponent. Prediction of team victory is based on this strategy. A runner may be matched against an opponent he may not be able to defeat; however, the runner's purpose here is to let no other opponent pass him by even though he does not defeat his match up. Matching up has been used more in recent years. It can provide a definite advantage in meets where teams are fairly close in ability levels. One disadvantage is that a psychological letdown can occur if a runner is unable to maintain his match up.

Change of Pace

This can be used as a team or individual tactic and is especially effective on the home course which should be most familiar. Some of the ways a change of pace can be employed are as follows:

1. Use Fartlek type running to confuse or demoralize the opponent.
2. Have a bunch or group pass weaker opponents at a faster rate of speed.
3. Increase speed on the uphill running, hoping to either fatigue or gain distance on the opponent.
4. Increase speed at certain points on the course where the opponent may lose sight of the runners ahead of him. (Examples: sharp curves or turns, the crest of a hill, wooded areas, corners, etc.)

5. Use a quick change of pace to check out the opponent to see what he has left or if he will accept the challenge.
6. When passing an opponent, change to a faster pace and gain enough distance on him so he cannot repass you at his present pace.
7. Sprint to certain parts of the course that are narrow and where passing is impossible. If a runner is beaten here, he may lose ground that he will be unable to make up later.

The change of pace tactic should be used to your team's advantage, not to your opponent's. Bluffing may work occasionally, but more than likely will backfire if the opponent regains the distance or employs similar tactics.

Lead Man Out

This is the use of individual strategy when a team has an outstanding runner who is capable of placing first in the meet. The lead runner will concentrate only on winning the race. The rest of the team may use other assigned tactics. The lead man out is effectively used with bunching or matching up by the rest of the team.

Boxing

Boxing is a tactic employed by two or more runners to stop an opponent from passing until such a point when they can out distance him to the finish line. The box consists of a man running in front of the opponent and another man to the best passing side. Another type of two man box is to put two runners in front and split the opponent, not allowing him to break through the gap. A three man box puts a man on either side of the opponent. Of course, the box must be legal and if the opponent is capable of outrunning the box, he will probably do so. However, boxing will make it more difficult and tiring. The legal box often results naturally in running conditions and is not planned, but should be recognizable to the runner when it presents itself. The box men must make it as difficult as possible for the opponent to pass on the easier parts of the course. They must face challenges, change pace, check out, and fight off the man trying to pass. Their positions in the box may also frequently change as the course changes. Boxing is most important versus a strong opponent or if the final finishing places will determine the meet. The box men must decide when to break and make the all out effort to the finish line (Illustration 3-1).

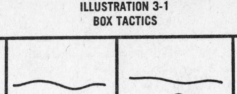

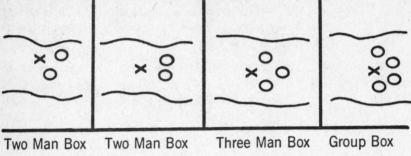

Two Man Box   Two Man Box   Three Man Box   Group Box

Passing

The key to successful passing is to pass the opponent and gain enough distance so that he cannot repass without a change of pace. If a runner can pass and only maintain a stride length or so, it may be better to wait until the runner is confident that he will not be repassed. When passing even the slowest of runners, one should accelerate so as to give the impression that there is no strain. Have your runners keep the best passing areas in mind when checking out the course. Avoid narrow areas where one cannot pass or can be boxed. Boxing can cause mental stress and upset the runner. Before entering trails or woods, the runners should take the initiative and pass opponents so they can have the advantage. If attempts to pass are challenged and the runner is unable to pass, have him stay close and check out the opponent's condition as well as his own. Another attempt may succeed or it may take your runner out of contention. If the passing runner cannot keep up the pace, he probably should not have passed at all. Another factor to consider is how much distance is left to the finish of the race. I have seen many a runner fight off challenge after challenge only to be out kicked in the last fifty yards of the race. Therefore, the knowledge of the runner's speed is also important. Passing may be an intense psychological battle between two close runners and it provides excitement and satisfaction.

Suggestions on Strategy for Runners

The following list of suggestions on strategy given to the runners can be helpful under competitive conditions.

1. Do not let the runner be taken out at the start at too fast a pace. He should know his pace and meet plan.
2. Do not project too far ahead. Take each opponent as he comes up. If the runner is in sixth position in a race, his next job is to move to fifth, then to fourth, etc.
3. Have the runner realize his potential, live up to it first and then improve it if possible. Do not run one half of a race in first position and then wind up last.
4. In extremely windy weather, take advantage of the drafting effect another runner can provide. Run a step or two behind and let him break the wind. Do not pass until he is showing fatigue and cannot keep up the pace.
5. Always be prepared for a sprint to the finish line. Do not take anything for granted even if the runner cannot hear or see an opponent.
6. Always run through the finish line. Do not pull up prior to it. Many runners have been nipped at the finish line by an accelerating runner who passed as they slowed down to cross the line. A good rule to practice is to always run past the finish line before decelerating.
7. Keep thinking while running. Think about race strategy and what the opponents are doing. Personal duals too early in the meet, unless planned, may hinder the team effort.
8. Always make sure the athletes are properly warmed up prior to the race.
9. Conserve energy by running as efficiently as possible.
10. Excessive mental stress can actually cause physical fatigue. Remember, the race is a product of the training; do not try to perform it in a different way.
11. Run the best terrain of the course possible, while maintaining the shortest route.
12. If an opponent shows signs of tiring, it may be a good time to pass him as this may finish him psychologically.
13. If a teammate is tiring, another runner may help him pick himself up. Talking, setting the pace, or running with him temporarily may do this. However, do not spend too much time and jeopardize your own position.
14. The runners should always know where they are in the race at all times.
15. Do not begin a finishing kick too early. Teach runners to acquire self-knowledge of their distribution of energy.
16. Each runner should possess some individual objective or goal for each race. It may be a faster time, a win, a higher place, a record, or defeating a certain opponent. This should not take away from the team competition, but should add to it as many of these goals do

contribute to the team effort. Often the individual goal is planned by the coach and athlete together.

In summarizing cross-country race strategies, it should be noted that they work best if planned ahead of time so the runners can assimilate them as part of their own mental preparation. Strategies given out in a pep talk form prior to the meet may only prove confusing. Strategies should be practiced in training to be effective in competition. A coach cannot expect his team to perform what he has not taught.

MEET PREPARATION

The organized coach should have many of the pre-meet requirements completed prior to the day of the meet. However, some items can be handled only on the day. The home meet differs from the away meet mainly in organization and the knowledge of the course.

Course Maps

A course map for away meets is a must. It is best if the map is received well in advance. The map then can be posted or copied so each runner has access to it. This will allow time for strategy and preparation. Course maps can then be filed and kept for future reference. If the map is not received at least a week in advance, the opposing coach should be contacted and a map requested.

A good policy for any coach to follow is to send out a meet schedule and a course map to each opponent as soon as possible after practice begins.

Knowledge of Course

Upon arrival at the opponent's course, at least one hour should be allotted to becoming familiar with the course. The opposing coach should have a tour of the course pre-arranged for your convenience. After the tour, the runners should be free to walk, jog, repeat, or study any part of the course they desire. If the course is new to the team and the coach, the coach may want to accompany his team on the tour. This is not a practice that need be limited only to new courses. Another aid in becoming famil-iar with an opposing course is to let the runners who have previously run the course help the new runners orient themselves to it.

Scouting

Scouting in person in cross-country is not essential and is usually not practical for most coaches. There are four other ways in which scouting can be handled.

1. Newspaper clippings of the opponents' meet results can be posted.
2. Many coaches will send out results of their meets to all of the opponents on their schedule. This is a real "gentlemen's" way of obtaining information about meets and often the coach who does this would appreciate reciprocation from his opponents.
3. The telephone can be used in contacting coaches who have previously run the opponent. Usually within a conference or a region, coaches will exchange information as they know they can do the same with you at a later date. This method is not underhanded or devious, because coaches will exchange information with more than one coach and about more than one team.
4. The best method of scouting is to form a newsletter within a conference, region, or among common opponents to which each coach will faithfully send his results for publication. The newsletter then can be sent out once weekly and kept on file. A small fee can be charged for the printing and mailing costs and the different coaches involved can yearly rotate the responsibility for the publication.

In the scouting report, the following information is needed to complete an accurate picture of how the meet went.

A. The meet score and scoring places.
B. The names of the runners of both teams who participated, their places and their times.
C. The date the meet was run.
D. The length of the course.
E. A brief course description.
F. The temperature and weather conditions.
G. The course record and its holder.
H. The present win and loss records of both teams.

Meet Plan

It is important to emphasize here that the strategy planned should not be a last minute detail. If enough scouting information is available, the coming meet should be planned out as soon as the previous meet is completed. The meet plan can be printed and handed out to the runners, but I have found that this is unnecessary when the race strategies are learned and practiced as part of the training. There may be a late change due to conditions that may occur and one must always allow for some flexibility. I have found the best time to state the strategy for the next meet is the first formal practice day after the previous meet. A critique of that meet can be accomplished as well as planning the race strategy for the coming meet. This strategy then must be worked into parts of the training schedule. Often, the amount of planning or strategy depends upon the caliber of the opponent to be run. When the meet is ready to start, a team should be completely ready. Last minute details can cause confusion and destroy the runner's state of mind.

Estimating the Opponents' Potential

As the head coach, you are not only responsible for the physical preparation of the athletes, but for their mental preparation as well. In the handling of cross-country runners, I have found complete honesty to be the best policy. Do not raise or lower opponents' times or lie about any other scouting information. An honest estimation of the opponents' potential and past performances is best. The dedicated runner will prepare himself for the meet to be run. Psychological preparation or the "psych factor" is important. If the athlete looses confidence in his coach's reliability to estimate the opponent, it can produce a negative effect on the "psych." There should be only a few meets per season in which the runners are led to a psychological peak. Some of my best team efforts have come from honesty in estimating a stronger opponent and honestly stating what we would have to do to win. No pep talk! Just plain facts. The athletes then took over and prepared themselves mentally for the task. This method often led to some outstanding victories over stronger opponents. The pre-meet atmosphere that prevailed was quiet and relaxed, yet one of intense personal involvement in the team effort.

Checkpoints

During the course tour or while conferring with the opposing coach, one should find out what checkpoints and mileage markers are available to the coach on the course. I definitely feel that in a course that does not repeat itself frequently the coach, if allowed, should make contact with the runners at least once during the race. Most major meets do not permit the coaches to follow the course as this could cause confusion. However, in dual or triangular meets, one and two mile checkpoints usually can be set up off the running course where the coach can obtain pace times and pass information to his runners. It is a definite advantage to see the runners throughout most of the race in order to evaluate their performance. I have used video taping in certain races for my own analysis and to show the runners how they performed. This method can prove most informative for all. While it is doubtful, once the race has started, if the coach is of much value to the runners, it is definitely important that he knows what is taking place.

4 *The Cross-Country Training Program*

THE TRAINING YEAR

Summer Training Program

The summer training program is most important to success in the fall. Contact should be maintained with your athletes. The best way to do this is by the use of letters. Often on the interscholastic level, team meetings could be held if they do not violate any conference or state rules. In any case, the letter from the coach can be a prime motivator for the athlete.

The summer program begins on July 1. A cover letter and a recommended training schedule should be sent out to arrive prior to that date. In this letter, encourage the runners to maintain personal contact with you concerning their training and progress as well as stressing the importance of the summer program.

A second letter and recommended training schedule is sent out for arrival prior to August 1. This should list the start and dates of the preseason training and the workouts to follow until preseason begins. Cover letters that are too emotional and inspirational at this time may tend to make the runner over anxious for competition and cause him too much mental stress in this early training.

A factor to consider in the training is what the athletes are doing for the summer. The type of work some may be involved in may limit their ability to complete strenuous schedules. Different situations will cause variation in the time and the physical effort they are able to put into it. The high school runner may have an advantage in his summer training since he is probably in his running environment with his coach near by.

The following are samples of July and August cover letters and recommended training schedules for those time periods. A realistic approach to summer training is best. To design workouts that are too strenuous or not feasible can do psychological damage if the runner is unable to complete them. It would be better to have the runner add to the workout rather than subtract from it.

JULY LETTER

Dear_____:

I hope you are having an enjoyable summer. With July rapidly approaching, it is time to start your physical preparation for the coming Cross-Country season. I am enclosing the training schedule for the month of July, and a meet schedule for the season. Preseason training is scheduled to start in late August. I'll send further details in my next letter as to the full agenda.

If you have any questions or problems concerning your training, feel free to contact me in person, by phone, or by letter. I am most interested in your progress!

The time to prepare for September is now. I cannot emphasize enough how important the summer training program is for success in the fall.

Good luck—I hope you are looking forward to the coming season with as much enthusiasm as I am.

Sincerely yours,

George R. Colfer
Coach of Cross-Country

JULY WORKOUTS (ENCLOSURE WITH JULY LETTER)

Our main concentration during this time is on building strength and stamina. We can accomplish this by:

1. LSD
2. Timed Distance
3. Fartlek
4. Strength Training—The Basic Program.

I want to emphasize that during this period of training, there should be no mental stress or pressure put upon yourself. Run and condition for fun! Make your workouts part of your daily life. You can train anytime, just fit it into your daily schedule. Once this is done, your training will become regular and any chance of missing a workout will be lessened.

Plan the training by the week. Put six training days per week into your schedule. Regardless of your time, the key to success is a good mental attitude. Remember MENTAL PRESSURE is much better AVOIDED—BE HAPPY!

Guidelines to Follow

1. Distance workouts should be from four to eight miles or thirty to sixty minutes in length.
2. Once weekly, take an LSD run of eight to ten miles.
3. In Fartlek runs, include striding intervals of 50 to 200 yards.
4. Strength train three times weekly using the Basic Program.
5. Total distance covered: 40 miles per week.

Sample Week

Monday—Timed Distance (40 minutes)	6	miles
Tuesday—Fartlek (Warm up-1/Fartlek-3/Cool Down-1)	5	"
Wednesday—LSD	7	"
Thursday—Timed Distance (50 minutes)	7	"
Friday—Fartlek (Warm up-1/Fartlek-4/Cool Down-1	6	"
Saturday—Rest	—	
Sunday—LSD	9	"
Strength Train—M—W—F Basic Program Total	40	miles

Another type of July workout would be for the runner who is competing with a track club or in open competition. Usually such organizations provide competition once weekly. A sample training week for the competing runner is as follows:

Monday—Timed Distance (45 minutes)	6½	miles
Tuesday—Fartlek (Warm up-1/Fartlek-4/Cool Down-1	6	"
Wednesday—LSD	5	"
*Thursday—Competition	4	"
Friday—Timed Distance (60 minutes)	8½	"
Saturday—Rest	—	
Sunday—LSD	10	"
Strength Train—M—F—Su—Basic Program Total	40	miles

*The four mile total is based on an average including the warm up, race distance, and cooling down period.

AUGUST LETTER

Dear_____:

Four weeks from today, we will be starting our first formal workout at 10 a.m. Our chance for a successful season is good. By now you should be ready to prepare yourself for the preseason training. I'm enclosing the agenda for preseason practice and the August training schedule.

You must now add to your weekly mileage and increase the length of your workouts. Your prior schedule and condition should make this task fairly easy. The average workout will be increased by about two miles daily.

Again, let's keep in personal contact concerning your progress and training.

I'm looking forward to an enjoyable and successful season.

Sincerely yours in Cross-Country,

George R. Colfer
Coach of Cross-Country

AUGUST WORKOUTS (ENCLOSURE WITH AUGUST LETTER)

Follow the same general philosophy and mental approach as suggested for July's workouts. Train six days per week and include the following:

1. Distance workouts should be from seven to ten miles or forty-five to sixty minutes in length.
2. Once weekly, take an LSD run of ten to twelve miles.
3. In Fartlek runs, include striding intervals of 100 to 300 yards.
4. In the distance workouts, include some terrain running.
5. Strength train two to three times weekly using the specific program.
6. Total distance covered: 50 miles per week.

Sample Week

Monday—Timed Distance (45 minutes)	6½	miles
Tuesday—LSD	8	"
Wednesday—Fartlek (Warm up-1/Fartlek-4/Cool Down-2)	7	"
Thursday—LSD	8	"
Friday—Timed Distance (60 minutes)	8½	"
Saturday—Rest	—	
Sunday—LSD	12	"
Strength Train—M—Th—(Sa) Specific Program	Total 50	miles

Both the July and August workouts are planned for the runner with some experience. Modifications can be made to any of the training schedules. By the use of guidelines instead of set programs, the coach can allow for the individual differences among his runners. Using this method, the coach and athlete can more easily plan the best workout to suit the needs and ability level of each runner.

The month of June is not considered part of the summer training program. Many teams are still competing in track in June with schools still in session. Since late May or June is the finishing period for a year of training and competition in cross-country and track, it is probably the best time to use as a rest or break period. This does not mean that the runner cannot train, but if he is exhausted or mentally fatigued, two to four weeks of rest from training can be beneficial. June workouts are not given for this reason. If the athlete wants to train, he can design his own workout for his needs and enjoyment and will probably welcome the opportunity to do so. If the athlete chooses to rest, he should be encouraged to remain mildly active in some other activity such as swimming, cycling, golf, or tennis.

NOTE: The following sample schedules presented for the preseason, early season, midseason, and late season training are designed for the experienced high school runner who has participated in a summer training program to prepare for the season. For the inexperienced or novice runner, modifications can be made to adapt the training to his needs and ability level.

Preseason Training

The preseason period is designed as an intense period of training to increase the build up of strength and stamina as well as beginning pace and interval work. During the preseason training, the runner should be concentrating only on his running. The high school coach may be able to set up some sort of training camp situation in which his runners can devote full time to training for about one week. This period is not only important to condition the athlete, but to build team morale. With no outside distractions, even if the runner sleeps and eats at home, the work during this initial period can prove invaluable.

The preseason period will extend past this first week and be in effect until five training days prior to the first regular season competition. Preseason training should be in effect for about 21 to 24 days. This period of training will usually give the highest mileage totals as without competition, all of the days can be devoted strictly to the training.

The following sample of a preseason training schedule is based on 21 days and includes preparation for the competitive schedule that was previously outlined in chapter 1. Required physical examinations should be given prior to the reporting date.

KEY TO ABBREVIATIONS FOR CROSS-COUNTRY TRAINING SCHEDULES

CCR	Cross-Country Relay	MAR	Marathon Run
CD	Cooling Down Period	OR	Orienteering Run
FK	Fartlek	PW	Pace Work
HR	Handicap Run	SpdT	Speed Training
HT	Hill Training	TT	Time Trial
IR	Indian Run	TD	Timed Distance
INT	Interval Training	Wup	Warm-up
LSD	Long Slow Distance	WKT	Workout

PRESEASON TRAINING
SAMPLE SCHEDULE FOR 21 DAYS

AM	Practice Day	PM
Wup - Formal WKT - 4 mile run. Check condition of runners. CD - Brisk 1 mile walk	1	Wup - Formal WKT - LSD - 5 miles CD - Brisk 880 walk ST - Maintenance program
Wup - Formal WKT - LSD - 5 miles SpdT - 6 x 110 CD - Jog 880 - Walk 880	2	Wup - Formal WKT - FK - 4 miles. Use change of pace running only. No interval runs. Jog last mile.
Wup - Formal WKT - LSD - 2 miles IR - 2 miles LSD - 2 miles SpdT - 7 x 110	3	Wup - Formal WKT - TD - 45 minutes using a training site with hills and terrain variety. ST - Maintenance program

Wup -	Formal	4
WKT -	LSD - 6 mile road run	
	SpdT - 8 x 110	

Wup -	Automatic - 2 mile run to training site
WKT -	INT - 2 x 660
	2 x 440
	2 x 220
	1 x 880
CD -	Run 2 easy miles

Wup -	Formal	5
WKT -	LSD - 7 miles on grass	
	SpdT - 9 x 110	

Wup -	Automatic - 1 mile run to training site
WKT -	INT - 4 x 880
	2 x 440
	1 x 1 mile
CD -	Run 1 easy mile
ST -	Maintenance program

Wup -	Formal	6
WKT -	TD - 50 minutes	
	HT - 6 x 60 yd Hill	

Wup -	Automatic - 1 mile run to training site
WKT -	INT - 4 x 1 mile runs
CD -	Run 2 easy miles

Wup -	Formal	7
WKT -	FK - 60 minutes. Include 1 x 880, 1 x 660, 1 x 440, 1 x 220, 6 x 60 yd hill, and 2 mile LSD run at end.	

Wup -	Individual
WKT -	LSD - 5 miles
	SpdT - 10 x 110
ST -	Maintenance program

End of First Week - Total Mileage = 84½

Wup -	Formal and Individual	8
WKT -	MAR - 15 miles measured road distance	

REST

SCHOOL BEGINS

REST		9

Wup -	Individual
WKT -	LSD - 7 miles
	SpdT - 11 x 110
ST -	Maintenance program

Wup - Individual
WKT - LSD - 5 miles
	10	Wup - Automatic - 1 mile run to training site
		WKT - INT - 6 x 440
		                6 x 220
		      PW - 2-mile run
		CD - Run 2 easy miles

Wup - Individual WKT - LSD - 3 miles SpdT - 12 x 110	11	Wup - Formal WKT - FK - 60 minutes. Use change of pace frequently. Include 8 x 60 yd hill, 8 x 55 yd sprint, and a 1-mile pace run. ST - Maintenance program

Wup - Individual
WKT - TD - 30 minutes
	12	Wup - Automatic - 1 mile run to training site
		WKT - INT - 6 x 660
		                6 x 330
		                4 x 220
		      IR - 2 miles
		CD - Run 1 easy mile

Wup - Individual
WKT - FK - 30 minutes
      Runner's choice
	13	Wup - Individual
		WKT - TT - 2 miles. Rest 15 minutes and repeat.
		      SpdT - 13 x 110
		CD - Run 2 easy miles
		ST - Maintenance program

REST	14	Wup - Individual WKT - OR - 12 miles. (Possibly plan picnic or cookout and invite parents, etc. The OR could be set up in a state park or other outdoor area.)

End of Second Week - Total Mileage = 83½

Wup - Individual WKT - FK - 30 minutes	15	Wup - Automatic - 1 mile run to training site WKT - INT - 8 x 880 HT - 800 yards of hill work CD - Run 2 easy miles ST - Maintenance program

Wup -	Individual	16	Wup - Automatic - 1 mile run to
WKT -	LSD - 3 miles		training site
	SpdT - 14 x 110		WKT - INT - 4 x 1320
			LSD - 3 mile run
			CD - Brisk 880 walk

Wup -	Individual	17	Wup - Formal and Individual
WKT -	LSD - 2 easy miles		WKT - Cross Country Relay Meet
	to fully loosen up		Each runner runs a 2 mile
	SpdT - 4 x 110		leg. (See chapter 2).
			CD - Run 2 easy miles
			ST - Maintenance program

Wup -	Individual	18	Wup - Automatic - 1 mile run to
WKT -	LSD - 5 miles		training site
			WKT - INT - 4 x 1 mile
			IR - 2 miles on hilly terrain
			CD - Run 1 easy mile

Wup -	Individual	19	Wup - Formal
WKT -	TD - 20 minutes		WKT - PW - 3 mile run
	SpdT - 15 x 110		INT - 2 x 880
			2 x 660
			2 x 440
			2 x 220
			LSD - 2 miles
			ST - Maintenance program

Wup -	Individual	20	Wup - Formal and Individual
WKT -	LSD - 2 easy miles		WKT - HR - home course distance
	to fully loosen up		(Emphasize all out effort.
	SpdT - 4 x 110		Base handicap on results of
			Relay Meet.)
			LSD -Run home course twice at
			easy pace. Reverse course
			the second time.
			SpdT - 16 x 110

	REST	21	Wup - Individual
			WKT - LSD - 12 mile road run in
			ability groups

End of Third Week - Total Mileage = 78 miles
End of Preseason Training Period

Early Season Training

The early season training is basically an extension of the preseason training except that due to the competition, the weekly mileage total is reduced. By this time, if not before, the team will have shown its potential and where its strengths and weaknesses lie. The training is now geared to prepare the runners for the early competition. Usually this period extends into the first two or three weeks of the competitive season. Meet preparation and race strategies become more important as part of the practice schedule. The summer and preseason training, if successful, should have the runners in good condition. Therefore, during the early season training, a "train—don't strain" concept should prevail. Practices should be carefully planned as to the apparent needs of the athletes and to the level of competition that is beginning. If competition is once weekly, the hardest practice days should be scheduled three and four days prior to the meet. Interval work should be used two and four days prior to the meet. The strength and stamina buildup can be maintained on the two days following the meet. It is important now to train the runners in ability groups and have those runners who will race together train together.

Two sample weeks of early season training for the 2-7-1 program and one sample week of early season training for the 2-7-more than 1 program are given (chapter 1, Table 1-1). For other types of programs, modifications will need to be made.

EARLY SEASON TRAINING
SAMPLE WEEK FOR TEAMS COMPETING ON SATURDAY

AM	Day	PM
REST	Sunday	Wup - Individual WKT - LSD - 12 to 15 mile road run ST - Maintenance program
Wup - Individual WKT - LSD - 3 miles SpdT - 16 x 110	Monday	Wup - Individual WKT - FK - 60 minutes. Use terrain similar to that of the coming meet. Run by ability groups. Practice race strategies. Experienced runners may help plan the Fartlek run.

Wup - Individual	Tuesday	Wup -	Automatic - 1 mile run to training site
WKT - LSD - 5 miles		WKT -	INT - Ladder Drill
			2 x 880
			2 x 660
			2 x 440
			<u>2 x 220</u>
			2 x 220
			2 x 440
			2 x 660
			2 x 880
			HT - 800 yards of hill work
		CD -	Run 2 easy miles
		ST -	Maintenance program

Wup - Individual	Wednesday	Wup -	Individual
WKT - FK - 30 minutes		WKT -	IR - 2 miles
Runner's choice			PW - Course distance ¾ speed
			LSD - 3 miles

Wup - Individual	Thursday	Wup -	Automatic - 1 mile run to training site
WKT - TD - 20 minutes		WKT -	INT - 4 x 1320
SpdT - 4 x 110			4 x 440
			PW - 2 miles - ¾ speed
		CD -	Run 1 easy mile
		ST -	Maintenance program

REST	Friday	Wup -	Individual
		WKT -	LSD - 3 to 6 miles
			SpdT - 4 to 6 x 110

REST	Saturday		MEET
		Wup -	Formal and Individual
			RACE
		CD -	Race distance or up to 3 miles

Weekly Mileage Total = 69½ to 75½ miles

SAMPLE WEEK FOR TEAMS COMPETING ON FRIDAY

	AM	Day		PM
	REST	Saturday	Wup -	Individual
			WKT -	LSD - 10 miles handicap run or orienteering run. (This workout is most important. The need here is for versatility and fun. The coach must provide the motivation for the workout.)
			ST -	Maintenance program
	REST	Sunday	Wup -	Individual
			WKT -	TD - 90 minute road run
Wup -	Individual	Monday	Wup -	Automatic - 1 mile run to training site
WKT -	LSD - 3 miles		WKT -	INT - 4 x 1 mile
	SpdT - 16 x 110			8 x 220
				HT - 800 yards of hill work
			CD -	Run 2 easy miles
			ST -	Maintenance program
Wup -	Individual	Tuesday	Wup -	Individual
Wkt -	LSD - 5 miles		WKT -	FK - 60 minutes. Use terrain similar to that of the coming meet. Run by ability groups. Practice race strategies. Experienced runners may help plan the Fartlek run.
Wup -	Individual	Wednesday	Wup -	Automatic - 1 mile run to training site
WKT -	TD - 30 minutes		WKT -	INT - 4 x 880
				8 x 440
				PW - Course distance ¾ speed
			CD -	Run 1 easy mile
			ST -	Maintenance program
	REST	Thursday	Wup -	Individual
			WKT -	LSD - 3 to 6 miles
				SpdT - 4 to 6 x 110

AM	Day	PM
REST	Friday	MEET Wup - Formal and Individual RACE CD - Race distance or up to 3 miles

Weekly Mileage Total = 70 to 76 miles

SAMPLE WEEK FOR TEAMS COMPETING MORE THAN ONCE WEEKLY

AM	Day	PM
REST	Sunday	Wup - Individual WKT - LSD - 12 to 15 mile road run. Include some hill training.
Wup - Individual WKT - LSD - 3 miles SpdT - 16 x 110	Monday	Wup - Automatic - 1 mile run to training site WKT - INT - 4 x 880 8 x 440 FK - 4 miles. Use terrain similar to that of the coming meet. Run by ability groups. Practice race strategies. Experienced runners may help plan the Fartlek run. ST - Maintenance program
Wup - Individual WKT - TD - 30 minutes SpdT - 8 x 110	Tuesday	Wup - Individual WKT - FK - 30 minutes Runner's choice
REST	Wednesday	MEET Wup - Formal and Individual RACE CD - Race distance or up to 3 miles

Wup -	Individual	Thursday	Wup -	Automatic - 1 mile run to training site
WKT -	LSD - 4 miles		WKT -	INT - 4 x 1320
				4 x 440
				IR - 2 miles
				PW - 2 miles - ¾ speed, practice race strategies, run by ability groups
			CD -	Run 1 easy mile
			ST -	Maintenance program

Wup -	Individual	Friday	Wup -	Individual
WKT -	FK - 25 minutes		WKT -	LSD - 3 miles
	SpdT - 16 x 110			

	REST	Saturday		MEET
			Wup -	Formal and individual
				RACE
			CD -	Race distance or up to 3 miles

Weekly Mileage Total = 67 to 71 miles

Midseason Training

Midseason training refers to the middle of the competitive schedule where the concentration of the meets is usually the heaviest. Rest may start to become an important factor here. Physical and mental fatigue should be closely watched and avoided. This often may be the time of the season when a runner becomes lackadaisical in his training. Rest may not always be the answer. Careful planning of the workouts and knowledge of the runners' past performances at this time of the season should provide the answers. The task here is to continue to build the runner toward his peak through the training and competition, yet not cause him to peak too quickly or suffer the effects of mental or physical fatigue. Variety and innovation in the workouts offer some remedies for these conditions.

The following sample weekly schedules for midseason training are given for both once weekly competition and for competition more than once weekly.

MIDSEASON TRAINING
SAMPLE WEEK FOR TEAMS COMPETING ONCE WEEKLY

AM	Day	PM
REST	Sunday	Wup - Individual WKT - LSD - 12 to 15 mile road run

Wup - Individual
WKT - TD - 20 minutes
      SpdT - 16 x 110
	Monday	Wup - Individual
		WKT - IR - 2 miles
		      FK - 3 miles
		      PW - 2 miles, ¾ speed
		      (the above are done continuously)
		CD - Run 1 easy mile
		ST - Maintenance program

Wup - Individual Wkt - LSD - 5 miles	Tuesday	Wup - Automatic - 1 mile run to training site WKT - CCR - split runners into teams of two, making homogeneous pairs. Each runner will run 4 x 1 mile. The rest interval will be his partner's run. Stress quality running. INT - 8 x 440 CD - Run 2 easy miles
Wup - Individual WKT - FK - 30 minutes Runner's choice	Wednesday	Wup - Individual WKT - PW - 6-8 miles at ¾ speed. Use terrain similar to coming meet. Run hills etc. as needed. If possible, run off roads on grass.

Wup - Individual
WKT - LSD - 3 miles
	Thursday	Wup - Automatic - 1 mile run to training site
		WKT - INT - 8 x 440
		            8 x 220
		      IR - 2 miles
		CD - Run 1 easy mile
		ST - Maintenance program

REST	Friday	Wup - Individual WKT - LSD - 2 to 3 miles SpdT - 4-6 x 110

REST	Saturday	MEET
		Wup - Formal and Individual
		RACE
		CD - Race distance or up to 3 miles

Weekly Mileage Total = 69½ to 72½ miles

SAMPLE WEEK FOR TEAMS COMPETING MORE THAN ONCE WEEKLY

AM	Day	PM
REST	Sunday	Wup - Individual WKT - LSD - 12 to 15 mile road run

Wup - Individual
WKT - TD - 20 minutes
SpdT - 16 x 110
	Monday	Wup - Automatic - 1 mile run to
		     training site
		WKT - PW - 2 miles - ¾ speed
		     IR - 2 miles
		     INT - 8 x 440
		CD - Run 1 easy mile
		ST - Maintenance program

Wup - Individual WKT - FK - 30 minutes Runner's choice	Tuesday	Wup - Individual WKT - TD - 30 minutes SpdT - 8 x 110
REST	Wednesday	MEET Wup - Formal and Individual RACE CD - Race distance or up to 3 miles

Wup - Individual
WKT - FK - 4 miles
Runner's choice
	Thursday	Wup - Automatic - 1-mile run to
		     training site
		WKT - INT - 4 x 1320
		          4 x 880
		          4 x 440
		CD - Run 1 easy mile
		ST - Maintenance program

Wup - Individual WKT - LSD - 2 miles SpdT - 16 x 110	Friday	Wup - Individual WKT - LSD - 3 miles

REST	Saturday	MEET
		Wup - Formal and Individual
		RACE
		CD - Race distance or up to 3 miles

Weekly Mileage Total = 64 to 67 miles

Late Season Training

Late season training is generally regarded as the final two to three weeks of the season, when the runners are being prepared for conference or other championship meets.

The runners must be mentally and physically ready at this time. Some athletes may tend to be overzealous about championships and unless the coach is watchful may become victims of overtraining. At this stage of the season, properly planned workouts and sufficient rest are important. A runner will not get into shape five days prior to a championship. However, he may be trained or peaked to run his best race at this time. Extremely fatiguing training such as hill work, stressful intervals, etc., should be avoided. A combination of distance work and proportionate intervals and speed work is best. If more rest than usual is indicated, by all means provide it. Individual differences among runners will show more at this time than during the rest of the season.

The following schedule is an example of a week's late season training in preparation for a championship meet.

LATE SEASON TRAINING
SAMPLE WEEK FOR LATE SEASON TRAINING

AM	Day	PM
REST	Sunday	Wup - Individual
		WKT - LSD - 12 - 15 mile road run
Wup - Individual	Monday	Wup - Individual
WKT - LSD - 3 miles		WKT - PW - Run course at ¾ speed.
SpdT - 16 x 110		Reverse direction and repeat
		CD - Run 2 easy miles
		ST - Maintenance program

Wup - Individual	Tuesday	Wup -	Automatic - 1 mile run to training site
WKT - FK - 30 minutes Runner's choice		WKT -	INT - 12 x 440 8 x 220
			LSD - 2 mile terrain run

Wup - Individual	Wednesday	Wup -	Individual
WKT - TD - 30 minutes		WKT -	FK - 5 miles SpdT - 16 x 110
		CD -	Run 2 easy miles

REST	Thursday	Wup -	Individual
		WKT -	PW/LSD - 8 mile run. Alternate miles with pace running and LSD
		ST -	Maintenance program

REST	Friday	Wup -	Individual
		WKT -	LSD - 3 miles SpdT - 4-6 x 110

REST	Saturday		CHAMPIONSHIP MEET
		Wup -	Individual
			RACE
		CD -	2 - 3 miles

Total Weekly Mileage = 64 to 67 miles

Off-Season Training

The off season is that period of time from the end of the cross-country season until the summer training begins. Most runners will naturally turn to indoor and outdoor track during this time. However, on occasion, a runner may not participate in track because the school may not have a track program, the runner may not be able to handle the regimentation of the track, or he may choose another sport during part or all of this time period. It is a definite necessity to keep active in running in one form or another. If for any of the above or other reasons, a runner cannot or does not choose to run track, he should be encouraged to keep running. Some ways in which this can be accomplished are as follows.

1. Develop an interest in marathoning.
2. Join and participate with an athletic or running club.
3. Perform off-season training with some older and experienced runners, who are road running, etc.
4. Set up an off-season training program for the athlete yourself. Keep a check on his program and workouts.
5. Participate in other sports which have high cardiovascular benefits, such as basketball and lacrosse.

While it is widely accepted that cross-country is most beneficial to track success in distance and middle-distance running, it should be noted also that the track season will benefit the runners in their future cross-country endeavors. Therefore, if at all possible, the running athlete should participate in both sports.

RELATED ASPECTS OF CROSS-COUNTRY TRAINING

Training for Different Courses, Terrains, and Distances

Throughout the season, it is possible to run on several different types of courses. Those most feared usually contain extremely hilly terrain, longer distances, or lack variety in construction and are boring to run. The home team should have a slight advantage on their own course, but more often than not, the better team will win on any course. When teams are equal in ability and condition, the home course definitely could be a factor.

Training for each course cannot be done two days before the meet. The coach should analyze what courses, terrains, and distances his team will be running before the preseason training begins. He then should use this knowledge when planning his training schedule. In other words, training for different courses, terrains, and distances should be part of the total program. For example, if extremely hilly courses are on your schedule, the hill training should begin early enough in the preseason to enable the runner to condition himself for the hills. If the hill training were just to begin four or five days prior to the meet, the runners would probably show signs of fatigue by meet time. However, if conditioned for the hills previously, they would not present a problem. The same would apply for longer courses or any other variables that would face your team. Crash programs for these situations will not prove as effective as a well planned total program to prepare for any situation that may occur.

Training the Day Before Competition

How to train the day before competition can become most controversial among coaches. Some of the training techniques for the day before a meet are:

A. Train as always (regular training day) except prior to difficult competition and championship meets.
B. Eliminate the AM workout, but run a regular PM practice session.
C. Eliminate the AM workout and reduce the PM workout.
D. Run one very light training session, usually in the PM.
E. Complete rest.
F. Run practice sessions of the same caliber as the coming meet.

Too much rest can be as detrimental as too little rest. If cross-country runners are given too much rest, they tend to become sluggish and inconsistent. However, reducing or tapering off the training has proven more beneficial before the meet than maintaining a full training session. One important point to mention about training before a meet is that whatever technique a coach adopts or believes in, he should convey its message to the runners. Cross-country runners tend to get into training habits and they must feel they are doing the right thing to prepare for the meet. If a coach is inconsistent or radical in his workouts the day before the meet, the runners may lose some of their psychological preparation. Techniques A and B are harsh but some coaches have used them with successful results. It is preferable to let the meet be a product of the training sessions. After all, competition in cross-country is the main reason for the rigorous training. As the previous training schedules show, the technique advocated here corresponds with technique D: to run one very light training session in the afternoon. The distance can be anywhere from one fourth to one half of the normal daily mileage. The techniques are LSD and some light striding. The distance is open ended (example—3 to 6 miles) to allow for individual differences among runners. The exceptions are in case of competition more than once weekly when a light morning workout may be included, and in late season training when more rest may be needed.

Training After Competition

The main reason for any jogging or running after competition is for cooling down purposes. If done, it should be easy running and relaxed.

Many coaches will leave this training optional to the athlete. It should never be used as punishment for poor performance. The high school runner may benefit more from this training due to the short race distance involved. The run itself should not exceed the race distance.

One good method for a training run after competition is to have the team re-run the course at an easy pace. This could be preceded by a brief critique of the meet. The runners would then run at a talking pace so they could discuss the course, the strategy used, and the outcome of the meet. This is a good time for the coach to jog along to discuss the race with the team if possible.

Peaking for Championship Meets

A definition of "peaking" is a well-planned training program, giving the runner what he needs most to prepare for a championship event. Guidelines to set this training are a knowledge of the runner, his past performances, his present condition, and the recognition of indicators as to his needs.

Peaking is mainly psychological if the runner is physically ready. The physical preparation must have taken place earlier. It is a combination of not being undertrained or overtrained. A runner must think he is ready as well as be physically prepared. Motivation is also important in peaking. A runner who has had individual success or is part of a successful team is more likely to reach this peak at the desired time.

Some coaches believe in training with just one or two meets per year in mind. Many coaches who adopt this concept will be disappointed. It is a technique that works well with great runners, but may leave the average runner frustrated. Possibly something such as this may be done with an outstanding runner in planning his individual goals for the season or with an exceptionally strong team, but setting the goals too high for the average or developing runner may lead to disappointment and even a lack of progress if some successes are not apparent.

The late season training offers a week's sample program for that period of time which includes the peaking for championship meets. However, as previously stated, peaking for certain meets involves much organization, planning, and preparation, beginning in the preseason training program and coordinating the training year with the competitive schedule to be run.

Cross-country is a sport in a realm by itself. While the coaching of cross-country may seem simple to the layman, it is a complex profession involving mental and physical preparation as well as organizational ability, planning, strategy, and a sense of individual abilities and needs. It requires a type of personality which can communicate with the athletes as well as provide them with the techniques for successful running.

The sport is most variable in method and technique. While certain qualities remain constant, the coach must be realistic about his program and the needs and abilities of his athletes. It is seldom that coaches agree on method and technique, and the reason is that they must always adjust to the athletes they coach and the program that exists within their school.

While most coaches agree that distance running is the best training for cross-country, there are many existing concepts on what will best complement this training.

5 Methods and Techniques for Coaching the Distance and Middle-Distance Events

The techniques and methods used in coaching the distance and middle-distance events are similar to those of cross-country.

In breaking down the events for training purposes, three categories can be utilized. One is for the athlete who runs two miles or above, one for the mile run, and the other for the 880. The main differences in training for each category are the mileage needed and the pace of the run.

THE SELECTION OF DISTANCE AND MIDDLE-DISTANCE RUNNERS

The first qualification for these events is a sincere love of running. Ideally, runners of all these events should be participants in cross-country, which would give them the distance buildup to move into the intensive training more quickly. Regardless of speed, cardiovascular endurance is most important to success in these events. Through interval training, speed and pace can be rapidly attained, whereas endurance cannot be built up quite as fast. Without a solid background of preliminary distance training, it is doubtful if an athlete can reach his full potential in these events.

CLASSIFYING TYPES OF RUNNERS

Classifying human performance is most difficult. However, the following character sketches may be an aid in helping the athlete compete in the distance he is best suited for.

The Long-Distance Athlete

This athlete loves to run. If he had his way, every workout would be an LSD or Fartlek type of run. He is usually a fine cross-country performer. He may be slightly negative towards pace or interval work and not enjoy the regimentation of the track. While independent, he possesses strong feelings for the success of the team. This may serve as a prime motivator towards the track competition. His individual successes may take different forms. While not possessed with outstanding speed, he will make up for it by conditioning and a healthy attitude towards competition. Marathoning and road running may be his off season interests. He may adapt to shorter distances, but chances are that trying to shorten his events may minimize his effectiveness.

The Mile Athlete

This athlete tends to be at home on the track with the faster training. Distance training may be a necessity to him rather than pure enjoyment. However, he is usually a consistent cross-country performer because of hard work and dedication. The mile is his run. He lives for it. He may be very competitive in practice situations and not be happy with less than perfection. This athlete is the pure thoroughbred in running; a combination of speed and endurance. Overtraining must be avoided as he will be most zealous during the practice sessions. He may be a natural leader because of his competitiveness and desire to excel. The main difference between him and the long-distance athlete may be running speed, as well as his preference for faster training.

The 880 Athlete

An athlete possessed with speed. He may or may not run cross-country, but if not, will perform the off season distance buildup. He will enjoy the shorter intervals and pace work. Too much distance work during the season may result in staleness. On the other hand, enough distance training is necessary for cardiovascular maintenance. Like his long-distance counterpart he may be independent, but is highly motivated towards success. Attempts to run longer distances may show poor results. Even though fast and in condition, he may lack the suitability for the longer events. The difference between him and the mile athlete is mainly running speed, and possibly a lack of the durability the miler possesses. However, many 880 athletes with proper training can perform the mile run well.

In applying these sketches to the high school athlete, it is not as important to identify with the actual performance of the runner, but the attitude and effort towards running that he demonstrates. All runners will not experience success in competition. However, they all will leave an impression on their coaches based on their attitude, effort, and performance.

A SCREENING TEST FOR BEGINNING RUNNERS

In selecting events for the beginning runner, the coach has to rely on his knowledge of the prospective athlete, even though it may be limited, and some sort of physical screening test. The following test should give an indication of the suitability of the prospect for the distance and middle-distance events. It is best used for beginning or untrained candidates. If the athlete has run cross-country, chances are you already know where his potential lies and this test would not be necessary.

The test should be taken at the beginning of the training period. Basically, it is an attempt to measure the amount of natural or untrained speed and endurance the prospect has. It should be noted that any screening test such as this is used to determine starting points, not end results. Prior to this test, the prospective runner should have passed the required medical examination.

1. Using the track, each prospect runs 880 yards. Record his time.
2. Walk a 440 yard recovery and rest for a total of ten minutes.
3. Using the track, each prospect now runs 220 yards with a standing start. Record his time.
   NOTES:
   A. Ask each prospect to give his best effort on both runs.
   B. Run the tests in groups of four.
   C. Run the 880 with an open start.
   D. Run the 220 in lanes.
4. Scoring:
   880 - If the prospect runs the 880 in:
      2:30 or less, rate him A
      2:31 to 3:00, rate him B
      over 3:00, rate him C

220 - If the prospect runs the 220 in:
   30 seconds or less, rate him A
   31 to 35 seconds, rate him B
   over 35 seconds, rate him C

5. Analysis:
   880—A rating of A in the 880 would indicate good probability for potential as a distance or middle-distance runner. A B rating does not indicate as much raw or natural talent, but through knowledge and training this runner may improve. A C rating indicates low cardiovascular endurance and probably a lack of natural talent for running.
   220—The ratings in the 220 would reflect on the runner's natural speed after a bout of strenuous activity ten minutes earlier. It is possible that this time may not be a true test of the runner's speed due to the fatigue involved, yet it will be indicative of his speed potential with the effects of fatigue approaching, which is pertinent to the distance and middle-distance runs.
   Regardless of his score in the 220, if the prospect scores a C rating in the 880, he should be put into an interim program of aerobic training combined with some light speed work for a period of two weeks and then retested. If a prospect were to score low in the 880 and then score high in the 220, his effort during the 880 would be more suspect than his condition. An example of an interim aerobic program for retesting purposes would be:
   A. Run 1½ to 3 miles at a moderate pace.
   B. 4-6 x 60 yards—acceleration stride and walk back to start.
   C. Workout five days per week.
   D. Retest after two weeks (ten workouts).
6. Starting Points. Those prospects who scored any combinations of A or B ratings should be placed in a beginning training program at this time. The best starting point for most runners is to train for the mile run. As the runner progresses or ability indicates, he may be moved up to the longer distance or down to the shorter distance. By starting with the mile training as a median, all events in the distance and middle-distance categories are within reach without any drastic changes in the type of training. The one exception to this would be the athlete who scored A ratings in both the 880 and the 220. His choice of a starting point for training could be either the mile or the 880.

SOME THOUGHTS ABOUT DISTANCE AND MIDDLE-DISTANCE TRAINING

The training program used by any coach should reflect a composite of his own philosophy and the needs and limitations of his total program. It is important to adopt a basis for the training. A training program that does not encompass the long-range goals of the total program may be self-defeating. While some may benefit, many runners will fall short of their goals and will not show the progress which should result from a well planned program. Workouts are limited in their benefits unless they are designed with the athletes' needs in mind and constructed according to the long-range goals that have been adopted. The training program for the track events is more regimented and more defined than that of cross-country. This is due in part to the variety of events and the use of the track as compared to the open course. Track is more methodical in its structure, specifically within each event. It is this concept that makes coaching more of an art than a science.

The Evolution of Distance Training Methods

When referring to the methods of distance training, they are generally the same as those described for cross-country in chapter 2. In tracing the origin and history of each method, one can see it is not the method that changes as much as it is the approach and technique with which coaches adapt it. Training methods generally evolve around the success that certain coaches and athletes have had with their use. Research into the areas of training and physiology also provide the basis for change.

The most notable and beneficial change of today is the better understanding of the aerobic needs of the distance and middle-distance runner and the realization that this need cannot be met in a short period of time. This has led to the idea of year around training and a greater emphasis on fall cross-country or off season distance training. Intensified interval, repetition, or speed training should not be attempted without a preliminary distance buildup as this could prove detrimental to the runner's performance and progress.

Quality or Quantity Running

This is one of the more controversial topics in distance and middle-distance training today. Quality running is often overshadowed by striving for a great amount of mileage. Its effectiveness in training after the preliminary distance buildup is probably second to none in preparing a runner for such events as the 880, mile, and two mile runs. Quality running is accomplished by the use of such techniques as interval training, repetition or pace work, and some forms of speed training. A well planned program of interval training is probably the best technique for effective quality running. Quantity running is the use of distance techniques such as LSD, Fartlek, or timed distance.

In summary, while a balance of both is needed in training, the quality type of running will work the athlete towards his optimum performance more quickly and efficiently after a period of preliminary distance training has been completed.

Two-a-Day Training

The same basic philosophy that was stated in chapter 1 concerning cross-country and two-a-day training is advocated here. The morning workouts and their purpose are generally the same, especially the point that it must be suited to the individual athlete and his needs as well as his durability. A further point of discussion concerning the use of two-a-day workouts for track is the recovery period in order to avoid the onset of chronic fatigue. With the use of quality running and more emphasis on speed and the pace of the run, caution must be taken so the athlete can fully recover to participate in the primary workout of the day, which in the school situation is usually in the afternoon. If a morning workout is feasible and desired, it should encompass a phase of training that will not be repeated in the afternoon. Most commonly, this would be the use of LSD, timed distance, or Fartlek for the AM workout. It would not be advisable to run back-to-back sessions of quality running. One psychological factor that may arise if a runner has been training twice daily and discontinues is the feeling that he is not performing enough work. There is no basis for this attitude as it is the caliber of the training that counts in track rather than the amount.

Weekly Mileage

The weekly mileage should be fairly comparable to that of late season cross-country training for the type of program being utilized (see table 1-1). The overall mileage will not be as high as for the cross-country season. As late spring and the height of the competitive track season is reached, it is quite possible to be training for the distance and middle-distance events on about 30 miles per week based on five training days, one competition day, and one day of rest. Other factors affecting total mileage would be the event the athlete is training for, whether or not there is an indoor competitive season, the climate and weather conditions, and the time of the season. For the high school runner, a rule of thumb for weekly mileage in the 880, mile, and two mile runs would be a total of 30 to 50 miles per week based on one workout per day and up to an additional total of 15 miles if morning workouts are used. Specific mileage for the different events and times of season will be stated in more detail in chapter 6.

How Much Competition?

With the use of the three season type of program, it is essential not to abuse track competition. One competition per week generally is sufficient. Many coaches will compete every other week in the early season, thus allowing for a two week training period between meets. If track is only an outdoor or spring sport, some coaches may choose to compete more than once weekly. In some colder climates, there may be only four to six weeks of suitable weather in which to run an outdoor track season. The answer, if at all possible, is to schedule an indoor season. For an indoor-outdoor track season running from January to June, the number of competitions should range from 12 to 16. This range should provide sufficient competition to challenge and maintain the runner's interest as well as allowing the maximum benefits from the training program.

Training the Day Before Competition

A light workout is recommended for the high school distance or middle-distance runner the day before competition. The purpose of this session is not conditioning, but to keep the athlete sharp and instill confidence for the coming race. If this workout seems to leave the athlete fatigued, chances are he is overtired from training or experiencing psychological fatigue. This session should be free from stress. Letting the runners perform it on their own with the coach present often proves successful. It also allows the coach more time for individual discussion or instruction. The following training session has proven successful for the objectives stated as well as popular with the athletes.

1. Take a one mile jog using the outside lanes of the track.
2. Use the usual flexibility or warm up exercises.
3. Run one-fourth of the race distance at the desired pace for the coming meet. (Example: for the mile run, this distance would be a 440, for the 880, it would be a 220, etc.) The purpose here is to let the runner feel the pace of the run and leave him eager to continue that pace.

4. Walk a brisk 440.
5. Stride 4 x 110 walking 110 between each run.
6. Jog 1 to 2 miles at a comfortable pace.
7. The runner should now be loose and relaxed, but not tired. The total distance covered should be about 2½ to 3½ miles.
8. Check out personally with the coach before leaving the track.

Exceptions to this training schedule are late season or prior to championship meets in which the coach's judgement would prescribe rest, and also in the early season if the coach would rather train his runners through some early meets.

Rest

During the early season training or before competition begins, a seven day training schedule may benefit the scholastic runner in his training endeavors. However, once competition is under way, especially in those programs that are three season or indoor-outdoor, a rest day for the runner is recommended. The high school runner is not fully mature and caution must be used not to overtrain him. As a college coach, I have seen a large number of good athletes who have completely lost interest in running or are burned out as a result of overstrenuous high school training programs. Choosing the time for this free day depends on the days on which competition is held. Since many schools now hold their meets on Thursday or Friday, the off day most likely would be a Sunday. For those teams competing on Saturday, it would mean not training the day after the meet, but chances are, it still would be better to leave Sunday free rather than lose a full training day by giving Monday off. If the runner really needs to loosen himself up, he could still do so at his own convenience. While many still advocate the seven day training schedule on a full year basis, I tend to disagree where the high school runner is concerned. During certain periods in the training year, a rest day at the appropriate time can be beneficial to a runner's progress.

Physiological or Psychological Fatigue

When an athlete shows fatigue in training and a lack of recovery from workout to workout, it is difficult to distinguish whether the athlete's fatigue is caused by physiological or psychological reasons. Physiological fatigue usually results from overtraining or intensifying the training before the runner is ready. In this form of fatigue, the runner is physically tired. It can usually be remedied by alternating or changing workouts, decreasing their intensity, or rest. Psychological fatigue is mind based. Many factors can cause this condition including personal, home, or school problems. However, relating more specifically to track, psychological fatigue can be caused by a lack of tolerance for the pain that is present in the training, disappointment in performance, or a lack of progress. The coach's main problem is to identify the type of fatigue and its cause. Once this is done, steps can be taken to correct the situation. Both types of fatigue show many of the same symptoms. Often an open discussion with the athlete concerning the problem can be the first step to eliminate fatigue. Occasionally, psychological fatigue may be present as a forerunner of physiological fatigue such as in the case of a runner who is pushing himself past his limit of tolerance. A quick diagnosis here may prevent the occurrence of physiological fatigue, which is usually the more serious condition of the two.

THE TECHNIQUES OF THE TRAINING PROGRAM

The techniques of training for the distance and middle-distance events are much the same as those discussed in chapter 2 pertaining to cross-country. While the priority of the techniques does change, their basic use and purpose does not.

The Basis of the Training Program

The training program for distance and middle-distance runners is based on a preliminary program of distance training for a build up of strength and stamina and interval training through the use of the set system. Other techniques used to complement the program are in-season distance training, repetition running, speed training, and strength training.

Warming Up

The type of practice to be run and the intensity of the training will often dictate the amount of warm-up. Before interval, repetition, or speed training, the athlete must be fully loosened up. Running is still the best method of warming up. Flexibility exercises will aid in preventing pulls or other injury prior to the faster training. The following exercise routine has proven useful after a running warm-up to prepare the runner for strenuous work.

1. Side Straddle Hop (Jumping Jacks)—12 repetitions. Use four counts per repetition. The exercise should be performed with a full range of motion at a medium rate of speed.
2. Squat Bender—10 repetitions, four counts. On counts 1 and 2, perform a deep knee bend and return. On counts 3 and 4, with the legs kept straight, bend forward, touch the toes, and return.
3. Windmill (Alternate Toe Touch)—10 repetitions, four counts.
4. Trunk Rotation—12 repetitions, four counts (6 to left, reverse, 6 to right). With hands on hips, feet apart, and legs straight, bend forward and rotate the upper torso in a circular motion.
5. Loosen up groin, knees, and ankles by individual stretching for 2 to 3 minutes.
6. Hurdler's Exercise—Bend forward 10 times and return. Lie back stretching the quadriceps, then pull the under leg to the chest. Repeat twice for each leg.
7. Sit Ups—12 repetitions.
8. Push Ups—12 repetitions.
9. Hamstring Stretcher—12 repetitions (6 to each leg), four counts. Cross one leg over the other and keep the legs straight. Start with hands on hips. On counts 1 and 2 bend forward, touch, and partially recover. On count 3 bend forward, touch and hold. On count 4 fully recover.
10. Side Straddle Hop—10 repetitions, four counts. These should be done with sharp movements and at a brisk rate of speed.

This routine or any other may be done on a formal or individual basis or at the completion of an automatic warm-up.

The Preliminary Distance Buildup

Running cross-country is undoubtedly the best method of building strength and stamina. In the case of the three season program, cross-country will generally carry the athlete into the indoor season. Many athletes in the distance and middle-distance events will be participants in cross-country. However, if an athlete chooses not to run cross-country and is not participating in another sport, he should be encouraged to run distance and strength train. A program of LSD, Fartlek, and timed distance leading the runner to a goal of five to six miles at a rate of seven minutes per mile or less is desired. If the athlete can perform this distance buildup, he should be able to move into the track training program. This should also be a maintenance goal of those who run cross-country during the interim and over the holidays prior to beginning track.

The major problem lies with the athlete who begins the track training without the preliminary distance buildup. This may occur with the beginner, the participant of another sport, or an athlete who neglects his distance training. Regardless of the reason, this runner is not ready to train with those who have the distance background. In my experience at both the high school and college level, there is very little chance of success for the runner who lacks the preliminary distance buildup. A four week program of preseason distance training which has proved successful in helping distance and middle-distance runners who lack the distance buildup or for one reason or another have had a training layoff is as follows. I do not offer this program as substitute for cross-country or off-season distance training, but as an alternative for those who lack the distance buildup. Modifications can be made if needed to fit the athletes' fitness level. It is important that this buildup be a gradual process.

PRESEASON DISTANCE WORKOUTS

1st Week

1. Run at a moderate rate of speed for 20 minutes—5 days (Mon.-Fri.).
2. Stride 220—jog 220, repeat continuously x 2—4 days (Mon., Tu., Thurs., Fri.).
3. Strength training program—3 days (Mon., Wed., Fri.).

2nd Week

1. Run at a moderate rate of speed for 30 minutes—5 days (Mon.-Fri.).
2. Stride 220—jog 220, repeat continuously x 3—4 days (Mon., Tu., Thurs., Fri.).
3. Strength training program—3 days (Mon., Wed., Fri.).

3rd Week

1. Run at a moderate rate of speed for 40 minutes—5 days (Mon.-Fri.).
2. Stride 220—jog 220, repeat continuously x 4—4 days (Mon., Tu., Thurs., Fri.).
3. Strength training program—3 days (Mon., Wed., Fri.).

4th Week

1. Run at a moderate rate of speed for 50 minutes—5 days (Mon.-Fri.).

2. Stride 220—jog 220, repeat continuously for 2 sets x 3 (total of 6 with a 440 walk interval between each set of 3)—4 days (Mon., Tu., Thurs., Fri.).
3. Strength training program—3 days (Mon., Wed., Fri.).

Notes

1. Run distance outside whenever weather permits.
2. Run the distance off the track, but perform the stride and jog (change of pace running) on the track if possible.
3. On Wednesday of each week, substitute a set number of miles (LSD) for the timed distance. This mileage should be comparable to the running time for that week.
4. At the completion of this program, the next two weeks should follow a hard day-easy day approach. Do not put the runner into an intensified program until he is ready.

In-Season Distance Training

Distance training during the track season should not be overlooked or substituted for with excessive quality work. While the preliminary distance buildup is most important, a combination of distance training and quality running will benefit the athlete. In-season distance training can be performed through the use of LSD, timed distance, or Fartlek. Fartlek training is popular mainly because it offers variety and change of pace running. Its main objective is the maintenance of strength and stamina as well as providing the athlete with a form of restful running to aid in the recovery process. Distance training can also be psychologically motivating. It is a good time to reflect on running as well as prepare for or recuperate from interval or repetition running. Depending upon the time of the season and the type of workout, in-season distance training will account for about 50 to 75% of the total weekly mileage for the distance and middle-distance runner.

The Set System of Interval Training

A general definition of interval training is a period of work or exercise followed by a prescribed recovery interval. Application of this definition to the running events implies a measured run with a measured recovery. There are several techniques that may be used in planning interval training workouts. These are generally organized according to the following variables.

1. Distance or duration of the run.
2. Speed or intensity of the run.
3. Number of repetitions of the run.
4. The length or duration of the recovery interval.
5. Nature or type of the recovery interval.
6. The frequency of the interval training sessions.

It is no secret that the success of the runners will depend on the coach's ability to combine these variables in planning the interval workout.

Benefits of Interval Training

When employed wisely, interval training offers many diverse benefits to the runner. These are aimed mainly at bettering meet performances, but also enable the athlete to accelerate more rapidly towards his potential.

1. Interval training provides more work with less awareness of fatigue.
2. More of a challenge is provided for the athlete.
3. Quality over quantity work is emphasized.
4. Competitive conditions are simulated.
5. Interval training permits rapid progress. Goals are more accurately planned and measured.
6. A personal approach to training is followed.
7. This method of training requires less time and space. While running at faster rates, more work can be accomplished in shorter periods of time.
8. Flexibility in training is allowed. Workouts can be changed quickly if needed. A well-planned program will prevent overfatigue as a result of training.
9. It is more beneficial to speed and anaerobic development.
10. Aerobic benefits and heart stroke volume may be gained in a shorter period of time.
11. The recovery interval avoids excessive accumulation of fatigue products in the circulatory and cardiovascular systems.
12. A great deal of the research supports the theory that a proper work-recovery ratio is important to successful training.

The Set System

The use of sets for interval training has several advantages over other techniques. There is greater consistency in the work performed and the measurement or analysis of the work is quite simple. Sets shorten the training time as well as make the workouts seem faster and easier to the athlete. Since consistency of the times of the runs is most important, there is less pressure or stress to record great times in practice. The challenge of the set to the runner is: Is he able to repeat the designated workout pace for each interval run of the set? In other words, can he post consistent times? Proper results require serious planning by the coach as well as knowledge of the individual abilities of his runners. Athletes in the same events can work the set together even if their workout paces are different. Competition should not be emphasized except to maintain consistency of the workout pace.

Another objective of the set system is to allow the runner to work towards his goal pace as quickly as possible. For example, if a 4:20 miler (440 race pace = 65 seconds) has a goal of a 4:12 mile (440 goal pace = 63 seconds) his workout pace for a set of 440's should be between 63 and 65 seconds, which will enable him to practice closer to his goal pace. Improvement will only occur when the quality or intensity of the work is increased or the recovery interval is decreased.

To plan a specific workout using sets, the components of the set must be analyzed. Each set should consist of the following:

1. A designated number of runs.
2. A designated distance for each run within the set.
3. A timed recovery interval, which should be adhered to strictly.
4. A designated workout pace for each run within the set.
5. A rest period following the completion of the set.

Types of Sets

The most efficient type of set is that of repetition of the same running distance within the set. An example would be 4 x 440. The advantage of this is to establish consistency in the pace. The ladder set would mix different distances in the same set. An example would be 2 x 330, 2 x 440, and 2 x 660. The ladder offers variation in training and in some cases will allow a more flexible approach to interval training. It should be mentioned that in a ladder set, each distance run should be repeated at least once to offer some consistency in the analysis of the work.

Number of Sets

Due to different stages of training and individual differences in ability, it is not possible to say exactly how many sets should be included in a workout. This must be the coach's decision. Sets may be combined using those of the same distance, of different distances or the ladder type to fit the needs of the training program. An example would be 3 sets to the workout in which set 1 is 4 x 440, set 2 is 4 x 330, and set 3 is 6 x 150.

Rest Periods Following Completion of a Set

After completion of the last run of a set, there should be a rest period of four to five minutes before moving on to another set or a different phase of the workout. Runners should walk during the rest period. Its length will depend upon the intensity of the workout.

Number of Runs Within a Set

A set should consist of no less than three runs and a maximum of eight. Since this training is intense and fatigue should be avoided, it would be more beneficial to increase the number of sets rather than surpass the maximum number of runs for a set. Runs of shorter duration would tend to be used in greater numbers. Using this concept, the quality of the training would not be affected. The distance of the event for which the training is being used should also be considered.

Distances for the Set System

While almost any distance can technically be put into a set, the quality of the work desired can best be obtained if the runs are kept to a maximum of 660 yards. The distances selected should depend largely on the events for which the training is planned. The 440 is a popular interval distance for the distance and middle-distance events, while 330's, 220's, and 150's are used for the shorter events. The most common distances used in the set system are: 660 yards, 600 yards, 550 yards, 440 yards, 400 yards, 352 yards, 330 yards, 300 yards, 220 yards, 150 yards, and 110 yards. The total duration of the run for set intervals should not exceed 120 seconds and preferably should be reduced as the runner's condition improves.

Recovery Intervals

It is important to emphasize again that the designated recovery interval should not be extended. If an athlete is not able to post consistent times, the workout pace should be lessened, not the recovery interval increased. The desired maximum recovery for any run should not exceed 120 seconds, while the minimum should be no less than 30 seconds.

Beginning runners may need additional recovery time in the initial training stages.

Deciding upon starting recovery lengths will depend on the condition and ability of the runner. As a rule, it would be better to start at recommended maximums and decrease as the runner's status changes. The maximum recovery intervals are recommended for the following distances:

LENGTH OF RUN	MAXIMUM RECOVERY LENGTH
660 yards	120 seconds
600　"	120　"
550　"	120　"
440　"	90　"
400　"	90　"
352　"	75　"
330　"	75　"
300　"	75　"
220　"	60　"
150　"	60　"
110　"	60　"

While some recovery intervals do not allow much time, it is best if the runner keeps himself mildly active during the pause.

Workout Pace (Speed of the Run)

The pace should be established depending upon the ability and condition of the athlete. It should be realistic and attainable. As the status of the runner changes, the pace should be adjusted. In most instances, the pace for a set interval run should be equal to or slightly faster than that of the same distance during a continuous run. A good method for checking the physiological effects of the run is to check the pulse rate of the runner at the end of the recovery interval. If the pulse rate exceeds 140, the workout pace should be lessened. This adjustment is effective in the case of beginning runners and during early season training. However, in advanced runners an allowance should be made for individual differences; therefore, this should not be an absolute rule.

Planning the Set

Through the use of the basic variables of interval training, the accompanying chart, Table 5-1, shows the different methods of planning a set workout. These methods can apply to a single set or a combination of sets. Proper planning of each set will allow for individual differences in ability as well as adding variety and flexibility to the training. The athlete should be able to work toward his goal at a faster rate of progress and with less chance of mental fatigue.

There is no definite order or progression. Combinations other than those given can be used; however, it is not advisable to change too many variables at any one time. Best results are usually obtained by a single change. Crash programs should be avoided.

TABLE 5-1

METHODS	DISTANCE	SPEED	NUMBER OF RUNS PER SET	RECOVERY	NUMBER OF SETS
STARTING METHOD	SAME	SAME	SAME	SAME	SAME
1	SAME	SAME	SAME	SAME	INCREASE
2	SAME	SAME	INCREASE	SAME	SAME
3	INCREASE	SAME	SAME	SAME	SAME
4	SAME	INCREASE	SAME	SAME	SAME
5	SAME	SAME	SAME	DECREASE	SAME
6	DECREASE	INCREASE	SAME	SAME	SAME
7	SAME	INCREASE	SAME	DECREASE	SAME

Example

Starting Method. A runner begins with two sets of 4 x 440 with a workout pace of 65 seconds and a recovery length of 90 seconds. When planning a change in the workout as progress demands, the coach may use one of the following:

Method 1. The distance, speed, number of runs, and the recovery length remain the same. The number of sets would be increased.

Method 2. The distance, speed, recovery length, and number of sets remain the same. The number of runs would be increased for each set.

Method 3. The distance of each run would be increased for each set. The speed, number of runs, recovery length and number of sets remain the same.

Method 4. The distance, number of runs, recovery length, and number of sets would remain the same. The speed of each run would be increased.

Method 5. The distance, speed, number of runs, and number of sets remain the same. The time of the recovery length would be decreased.

Method 6. The distance would be decreased, while the speed of each run is increased. The number of runs, recovery length, and number of sets remain the same.

Method 7. The distance, number of runs, and number of sets remain the same. The speed of the runs would be increased and the recovery length decreased. This method would produce the greatest change in the intensity of the workout.

In conclusion, it is apparent that the success of the set system depends upon the ability of the coach to organize the training program. A review of the important factors that must be taken into consideration are:

1. An adequate knowledge of interval training.
2. A period of preliminary distance training.
3. The integration of interval training into the total program.
4. Planning of the set workout:
   A. Emphasizing quality over quantity work.
   B. Suiting the training to the ability level of the athlete.
   C. Use of the analysis of the training.
   D. Patience in reaching goals and training levels.
   E. Making the workouts pertinent to the events for which the training is used.

Repetition Running

Repetition runs are a form of quality running. This technique is very similar to interval training except for the length of the run and the length of the recovery interval. While repetition running is less stressful than interval training, it still should be well planned, especially when choosing the speed of the run.

The repetition run is longer than the interval run as is the recovery period. The speed of each run should not exceed the present race pace of the runner for that distance and often may be slower. If used as an overdistance run, the pace must be adjusted to produce oxygen debt and challenge cardiovascular endurance, but definitely should not be an all out effort.

The length of repetition runs usually is between 440 yards and one mile for the distance and middle-distance events. Many repetition workouts are run at one half of the race distance. The number of repetition runs per workout should be equivalent to that of the interval set system depending on the length of the run and the intensity of the workout.

The interval between each run should be sufficient to insure near complete recovery. The length of the rest period may be from three to eight minutes depending on the length of the run. The recovery should be walked.

Repetition running is often used as a variation and in conjunction with interval training. Its emphasis is on longer runs and overdistance in the early season and shorter runs in mid and late season.

The Use of Speed Training

While the entire training emphasis is on producing sufficient speed for the pace of the run, additional speed work needs to be added to the program. This can take two forms. (1) The use of speed improvement programs as discussed in chapter 12. (2) Speed work in the training program which requires the athlete to run or sprint at a pace considerably faster than his race pace.

Speed work is quality work. Some type of speed training should be included at least once per week in the training program since speed is specific to the task. The distance of the speed run should be between 50 and 120 yards for the distance and middle-distance events. Two types of speed workouts which seem to accomplish the objective for the track training are as follows:

1. *Sprint and Jog.* Using the track, run 110 yard acceleration sprints with a 110 yard slow jog in between runs.
2. *Sprint and Walk.* Using the track, run 110 yard full sprints with a 110 yard walk in between runs.

Both of these workouts should be taken near the completion of the workout, but not when the runner is near fatigue. Method #1 is used best with interval or repetition running. Its continuity does not allow full recuperation, therefore the athlete unknowingly will have to concentrate more on his running posture and mechanics. Method #2 best follows a distance workout or a sustained running effort. By asking for a full effort on the sprint and allowing a rest period, near maximum effort should be exerted. The total sprint distance for any workout should not exceed 1000 yards and this only for a well-conditioned runner.

Training Up and Training Down

These are two training techniques which can produce variety in the workouts as well as provide benefits for the runner.

Training up means to move the runner's training for that session up to the schedule for the next longer event. Training down is to let the runner train with the next shorter event for that workout. Examples for the 880 runner would be to train with the mile or two milers (up) or with the 440 athletes (down). Up training is used when the need is for more distance or longer distances of quality work. Training down is beneficial to the pace of the run and working with faster athletes. These techniques should only be used when needed and not on a random basis. In a normal situation, a runner may benefit from one or the other technique in about one out of every ten training sessions.

Time Trials

It has been stated by many coaches and great runners that a full effort time trial is a waste of time and energy. If a poor time is posted, it is psychologically defeating and a good time is wasted effort since it does not count. Through the use of quality running techniques, it is fairly easy to predict the runner's potential at a certain date. A time trial may benefit the less experienced or novice runner by simulating race conditions and giving him the chance to explore his present condition.

There are numerous ways in which to accomplish the objectives of a time trial through achievement runs. Some of the more successful ones are as follows.

1. Run ¾ of the run at race or goal pace. Finish the remaining ¼ at half speed.
2. Run an over-distance time trial at about ¾ speed.
3. Run a time trial for ½ of the race distance. Rest and repeat the trial again.
4. Run ½ of the race distance at race pace. Jog the other half. Repeat this again without stopping.
5. Back-to-back time trial. Run the race distance at ⅞ speed. Rest, then repeat the run once more. Consistency in the two times is the goal.

Cooling Down

Cooling down after training sessions is most important to the track athlete. Often the cooling down from long-distance running happens automatically. If the athlete is fatigued from quality work, a period of walking followed by a jog may offer the most benefit. The cooling down should not be stressful. As stated in chapter 2, the runner should recuperate from fatigue and nearly return to the pre-exercise state as a result of the cooling down period.

Strength Training

Strength training should be a regular part of the training program. In chapter 11, complete programs for the distance and middle-distance runner are given. The use of strength training as a supplement to the running program should not be underestimated.

RACE STRATEGIES

The organization for race strategy consists of planning the competition, knowledge of the opponent, deciding upon a race plan, and the tactics to be used. Scouting the opponents can be accomplished in the same manner as described in chapter 3 for cross-country. Once the coach has decided upon the race plan and tactics to be used, he should inform and discuss the plan with his runners. Use individual conferences or team meetings for the presentation of this information.

The Race Plan

The race plan should be formulated by considering the following factors:

1. Distance of the race.
2. Type of race (dual meet—invitational—championship).
3. Time of season.
4. Race objective.
5. Ability of the opponent to be run.
6. Present ability level and condition of the runner.
7. Maximum and minimum running pace at which the runner can lead, follow and win, or accomplish the race objective.

By using these factors as a guide, the coach can objectively decide upon a plan for each participating runner. If the athlete is experienced and mature, he may be of assistance to the coach in the preparation of the race plan.

Pacing the Run

Pace judgement is a characteristic of the experienced and successful runner. Each runner must learn pace judgement. In distance and middle-distance racing, it is not a physical or inherent quality. The novice runner tends to start too fast, creating oxygen debt, which causes a slowing of the pace and usually results in an ineffective run. Pace judgement should be practiced during the workouts. Interval training and repetition runs help in pacing by working nearer to the race pace and establishing a pace knowledge. For longer intervals and repetitions, split times from the runs will also help in pace judgement.

For the distance and middle-distance races, a consistent or even pace throughout the race is best. This can vary between 1 and 3 seconds per 440, but anything over 5 seconds would be considered unstable or erratic.

Example: For a 5 minute mile, the breakdown would be:

440 = 75 seconds
880 = 2:30
1320 = 3:45
MILE = 5:00

However, an unacceptable race using good pace judgment may look like this:

440 = 73 seconds
880 = 2:29 (76)
1320 = 3:46 (77)
MILE = 5:00 (74)

Varied Pace

Using a varied pace during a race is not generally recommended for the scholastic runner since it is quite physiologically and psychologically demanding. It is an aggressive type of running usually characterized by never relinquishing the lead. By the use of Fartlek running and fighting off all challenges, the runner hopes to exhaust his opponents and destroy them psychologically. However this can "backfire" in which case the runner may take himself out of contention. The athlete attempting this strategy would need to be a strong runner and capable of running a good race in which case he may perform better using an even pace.

Speed

The speed of a runner in the distance and middle-distance events is most important during the finishing phase of the race. Obviously, if all other factors are equal, the faster man will win. A runner should possess knowledge of his speed for tactical use as well as knowing or estimating his opponent's speed to be able to judge his finish and plan the race accurately. It is a sad sight to see a good runner lose a race by being out-kicked at the finish line knowing he had reserve strength left, but not sufficient speed. Speed can be improved. Chapter 12 offers a variety of speed improvement programs.

RACE TACTICS

Any race tactic used should be controlled by a distribution of energy to be successful. The race tactic is simply a plan of action for competition. Often it is based on the race objective. The purpose of most tactics is to make the opponent vary from his pace or to exploit a trait the runner possesses such as a strong finishing kick.

Front Running

Possibly the easiest of all race tactics, front running is accomplished by taking the lead in a race as soon as the pace is established. However the front runner is not setting the pace for anyone else. His goal is to place distance between himself and his opponents as quickly as possible. Front running requires confidence. One point of caution is not to be taken out too quickly by a pace setting or ''rabbit'' runner. This tactic is exceptionally good for the runner who lacks a strong finishing kick.

Running Behind

This tactic is best employed by the runner with a strong finishing kick. It also is useful in checking out the opponent's condition or if little is known about the opposition. It may be used to counter a front runner or the varied pace strategy. The point is to run closely behind the lead runner or the opponent to be defeated until the runner is confident that he can pass and not be passed in return.

Running behind may require more psychological preparation as there is always thought about the man ahead. However it may benefit the inexperienced runner who may not possess the physical ability or the confidence to attempt other tactics.

Time Tactic

The time tactic can be used in two ways. First of all, it is the most efficient tactic to use for a runner who wants to achieve his best performance in regard to time or a record. The time tactic requires precision planning to run a designated time. A fast steady pace must be held with little variation. The time tactic works well for the outstanding runner who is not getting quality opposition, in order to test his potential. The tactic is individual almost to the point of ignoring other runners in the race.

The second way to use the time tactic is for the runner who has little chance of placing in the meet, but is mainly running for experience and improvement. By planning a time objective, the race will have more meaning and offer an opportunity for one form of success.

It has been stated that this is the most efficient tactic in determining one's true potential.

Win Tactic

The win tactic emphasizes winning or placing as high as possible in the race. More specifically, the runner tries to win without any regard to the resulting time. The tactic relies on sensible pace judgement, distribution of energy, reacting to the competitive situation, and concentrating on the latter part of the race especially the kick to the finish line. One should never fall too far behind or be out of contention. The win tactic is natural to the scholastic runner.

It is widely accepted that race tactics are essential to successful performance. However flexibility should be allowed for before and after the race has started. It is impossible to completely predict human behavior and often winning may depend upon the ability to alter or change tactics during a race.

6 Training Programs for the Distance and Middle-Distance Events

ORGANIZATION OF THE PRACTICE SCHEDULE

Organization of the practice schedule for the distance and middle-distance events should be based on two factors, the present condition of the athlete and the time of the season. This would take into consideration the preliminary distance buildup, present training level, and the objective or goal of the runner. Workouts should be planned in accordance with the competitive schedule.

The practice schedule can be planned on a yearly, seasonal, monthly, bi-weekly, or weekly basis. A good method is to develop a training cycle to fit the season and the needs of the program.

Workouts can be planned starting with the first day of the cycle and progressing to the competition day or by starting at the competition day and planning in reverse to the first day of the cycle. Whichever method is selected, it is often beneficial to retrace the training cycle by the other method. This offers the coach more insight into his overall planning.

When conditions dictate, the coach should be flexible regarding the planned practice schedule. The needs and conditions for this flexibility parallel those presented for cross-country in chapter 1.

Adaptation to Indoor Running

Indoor running may present different conditions as well as different distances to the athlete. The 600 and 1000 yard runs can be additions to the regular 880, one mile, and two mile events. These runs offer variety as well as test distances for the 880 and mile athlete in competition.

Alteration or change in the training schedule is not necessary except for establishing pace knowledge of the indoor runs.

The adjustments to indoor conditions may include shorter, narrower tracks, curves or turns that may be difficult to negotiate, congested running, fewer passing opportunities, and different running surfaces. These conditions often make some of the strategy and tactics of running outdoors unsuitable. The shorter the race distance, the more important the runner's position becomes during the race. Often a poor position can cost the runner a race by forcing him to expend too much energy in attempting to catch up and pass the opposition.

Pace strategy is important in indoor running. A varied or change-of-pace tactic is needed to pass or hold off a challenging opponent at strategic points. The front running and win tactic may be the best race tactics to use in indoor competition.

The Steeplechase and Three-Mile Run

Presently, the steeplechase and three-mile run are not regularly scheduled interscholastic events. Since the training for the two or three-mile would basically be the same, the high school runner's transition to the college distance should not be too difficult. The steeplechase presents a different situation. This is an event of national and international competition. It would seem reasonable to run this event at the high school level, not only to gain additional exposure, but because the event is interesting, challenging, and fun. The steeplechase requires a different breed of distance runner. It requires strength, stamina, and hurdling ability. As in other events, some experience before the college level would enhance the potential of the future steeplechase athlete as well as offering another event for participation in the interscholastic track program.

TRAINING PROGRAMS FOR THE TWO-MILE, ONE-MILE, AND 880

The following training programs are presented for an indoor-outdoor season. They are based on training and competition from January to June. The number of days included in a training cycle is determined by the time of the season and the frequency of competition. The next consideration is the type of training day desired, or the approach to the training. Once these factors are established, the actual workouts can be planned for the cycle.

Types of Training Days

The type of training day is stated for the PM or primary workout. Whether the day is hard or easy etc. is based on the training techniques and the intensity of the workout. The training days are broken down into six categories as follows.

1. HARD DAY—Quality running: High intensity work; Interval training, Repetition runs.
2. EASY DAY—Quality or Quantity running: Low intensity work; Varied techniques.
3. DISTANCE DAY—Quantity running: Varied intensities; LSD, Fartlek, Timed Distance.
4. LIGHT DAY—Premeet workout or extremely light training.
5. ACHIEVEMENT DAY—Time Trials; Achievement runs; Pace objectives.
6. REST DAY—Complete rest; Loosen up; Strength train; Runner's choice.

NOTE: The training cycles and sample schedules presented are designed for the experienced high school runner who has participated in cross-country or had a preliminary distance buildup. For the inexperienced or novice runner, modifications can be made to adapt the training to his needs and ability level.

KEY TO ABBREVIATIONS FOR DISTANCE AND MIDDLE-DISTANCE TRAINING SCHEDULES

AM(workout)—Supplementary workout of the day
*CD—Cooling Down Period
FK—Fartlek
IR—Indian Run
INT—Interval Training
LSD—Long Slow Distance
PM(workout)—Primary workout of the day

REP—Repetition Run
RR—Road Run
S&J—Alternating Stride and Jog
SpdT—Speed Training
SSIT—Set System of Interval Training
ST—Strength Training
TD—Timed Distance
TT—Time Trial or Achievement Run
*Wup—Warm-up

*If the warm-up or cooling down period is not mentioned specifically in the workout, it is assumed that they are automatically contained within the techniques used in that training session.

DISTANCE AND MIDDLE-DISTANCE EVENTS
13-DAY TRAINING CYCLE FOR JANUARY

*Monday—HARD DAY
*Tuesday—EASY DAY
  Wednesday—HARD DAY
*Thursday—EASY DAY
*Friday—DISTANCE DAY
  Saturday—HARD DAY
  Sunday—DISTANCE DAY

*Monday—HARD DAY
*Tuesday—EASY DAY
  Wednesday—HARD DAY
*Thursday—DISTANCE DAY
  Friday—EASY DAY
  Saturday—ACHIEVEMENT DAY
  Sunday—REST DAY

*AM WORKOUT

SAMPLE TRAINING SCHEDULES FOR JANUARY CYCLE

TWO MILE	ONE MILE	880
MONDAY AM-LSD-2-3M PM-Wup-1M IR-2M INT-660x4 S&J-220/220x4 CD-2M	MONDAY AM-LSD-2-3M PM-Wup-1M IR-2M INT-440x4 S&J-220/220x4 CD-2M	MONDAY AM-LSD-2M PM-Wup-1M IR-2M INT-330x4 S&J-165/165x6 CD-2M
TUESDAY AM-TD-20mins. PM-FK-5M SpdT-110x8 CD-1M ST—Specific	TUESDAY AM-TD-20mins. PM-FK-4M SpdT-110x8 CD-1M ST—Specific	TUESDAY AM-TD-15mins. PM-FK-4M SpdT-110x8 CD-1M ST—Specific

WEDNESDAY
AM-OFF
PM-Wup-2M
 SSIT-(1)660x3
   (2)440x3
   (3)330x3
 S&J-220/220x4
 CD-2M
	WEDNESDAY
	AM-OFF
	PM-Wup-2M
	 SSIT-(1)440x3
	   (2)330x3
	   (3)220x3
	 S&J-220/220x4
	 CD-2M
		WEDNESDAY
		AM-OFF
		PM-Wup-2M
		 SSIT-(1)330x3
		   (2)220x3
		   (3)220x3
		 S&J-165/165x6
		 CD-2M

THURSDAY	THURSDAY	THURSDAY
AM-LSD-2-4M	AM-LSD-2-3M	AM-LSD-2M
PM-Wup-1M	PM-Wup-1M	PM-Wup-1M
REP-880x2	REP-660x2	REP-440x2
1320x2	880x2	660x2
CD-2M	CD-2M	CD-2M

FRIDAY	FRIDAY	FRIDAY
AM-Jog-1M	AM-Jog-1M	AM-Jog-1M
SpdT-110x8	SpdT-110x8	SpdT-110x8
Jog-1M	Jog-1M	Jog-1M
PM-FK-30mins.	PM-FK-30mins.	PM-FK-20mins.
TD-30mins.	TD-30mins.	TD-20mins.
ST—Specific	ST—Specific	ST—Specific

SATURDAY	SATURDAY	SATURDAY
AM-OFF	AM-OFF	AM-OFF
PM-Wup-2M	PM-Wup-2M	PM-Wup-2M
SSIT-(1)660x4	SSIT-(1)440x4	SSIT-(1)330x4
(2)660x4	(2)440x4	(2)330x4
FK-30mins.	FK-30mins.	FK-30mins.

SUNDAY	SUNDAY	SUNDAY
RR-12-15M	RR-10-12M	RR-8-10M

AM MILEAGE = 12½	AM MILEAGE = 11½	AM MILEAGE = 8½
PM MILEAGE = 59	PM MILEAGE = 51½	PM MILEAGE = 46½
WEEKLY TOTAL = 71½	WEEKLY TOTAL = 63	WEEKLY TOTAL = 55

MONDAY	MONDAY	MONDAY
AM-LSD-2-4M	AM-LSD-2-3M	AM-LSD-2M
PM-Wup-1M	PM-Wup-1M	PM-Wup-1M
REP-1Mx4	REP-1320x4	REP-660x4
S&J-220/220x4	S&J-220/220x4	S&J-165/165x6
CD-1M	CD-1M	CD-1M

TUESDAY	TUESDAY	TUESDAY
AM-TD-20mins.	AM-TD-20mins.	AM-TD-15mins.
PM-Wup-1M	PM-Wup-1M	PM-Wup-1M
IR-2M	IR-2M	IR-2M
SpdT-110x8	SpdT-110x8	SpdT-110x8
FK-30mins.	FK-20mins.	FK-15mins.
ST—Specific	ST—Specific	ST—Specific

WEDNESDAY	WEDNESDAY	WEDNESDAY
AM-OFF	AM-OFF	AM-OFF
PM-Wup-2M	PM-Wup-2M	PM-Wup-2M
SSIT-(1)660x4	SSIT-(1)440x4	SSIT-(1)330x4
(2)660x4	(2)330x4	(2)330x4
(3)440x4	(3)220x4	(3)220x4
S&J-220/220x4	S&J-220/220x4	S&J-165/165x6
CD-2M	CD-2M	CD-2M

THURSDAY	THURSDAY	THURSDAY
AM-Jog-1M	AM-Jog-1M	AM-Jog-1M
SpdT-110x8	SpdT-110x8	SpdT-110x8
Jog-1M	Jog-1M	Jog-1M
PM-LSD-10M	PM-LSD-8M	PM-LSD-6M
ST—Specific	ST—Specific	ST—Specific

FRIDAY	FRIDAY	FRIDAY
AM-OFF	AM-OFF	AM-OFF
PM-Wup-1M	PM-Wup-1M	PM-Wup-1M
S&J-220/220x4	S&J-220/220x4	S&J-165/165x6
FK-3M	FK-2M	FK-2M

SATURDAY	SATURDAY	SATURDAY
AM-OFF	AM-OFF	AM-OFF
PM-TT-3M overdis- tance run at 7/8 speed LSD-3M	PM-TT-1½M overdis- tance run at 7/8 speed LSD-3M	PM-TT-1M overdis- tance run at 7/8 speed LSD-3M

SUNDAY—REST	SUNDAY—REST	SUNDAY—REST

AM MILEAGE = 9½	AM MILEAGE = 8½	AM MILEAGE = 7½
PM MILEAGE = 43	PM MILEAGE = 36½	PM MILEAGE = 31½
WEEKLY TOTAL = 52½	WEEKLY TOTAL = 45	WEEKLY TOTAL = 39
13 DAY TOTAL = 124	13 DAY TOTAL = 108	13 DAY TOTAL = 94

DISTANCE AND MIDDLE-DISTANCE EVENTS
13-DAY TRAINING CYCLE FOR FEBRUARY

*Monday—HARD DAY
*Tuesday—EASY DAY
 Wednesday—HARD DAY
*Thursday—DISTANCE DAY
*Friday—EASY DAY
 Saturday—ACHIEVEMENT/HARD DAY
 Sunday—DISTANCE DAY

*AM WORKOUT

*Monday—HARD DAY
*Tuesday—EASY DAY
 Wednesday—HARD DAY
*Thursday—DISTANCE DAY
 Friday—LIGHT DAY
 Saturday—COMPETITION DAY
 Sunday—REST

SAMPLE TRAINING SCHEDULES FOR FEBRUARY CYCLE

TWO MILE	ONE MILE	880
MONDAY AM-LSD-2-4M PM-Wup-1M REP-1Mx4 S&J-220/220x4 CD-2M	MONDAY AM-LSD-2-3M PM-Wup-1M REP-1320x4 S&J-110/110x8 CD-2M	MONDAY AM-LSD-2M PM-Wup-1M REP-660x4 S&J-110/110x8 CD-2M
TUESDAY AM-TD-20mins. PM-FK-3M IR-2M SpdT-110x8 CD-1M ST—Specific	TUESDAY AM-TD-20mins. PM-FK-2M IR-2M SpdT-110x8 CD-1M ST—Specific	TUESDAY AM-TD-20mins. PM-FK-2M IR-2M SpdT-110x8 CD-1M ST—Specific
WEDNESDAY AM-OFF PM-Wup-2M SSIT-(1)660x4 (2)660x4 (3)440x4 CD-2M	WEDNESDAY AM-OFF PM-Wup-2M SSIT-(1)440x4 (2)440x4 (3)220x4 CD-2M	WEDNESDAY AM-OFF PM-Wup-2M SSIT-(1)330x4 (2)330x4 (3)220x4 CD-1M

THURSDAY	THURSDAY	THURSDAY
AM-Jog-1M	AM-Jog-1M	AM-Jog-1M
SpdT-110x8	SpdT-110x8	SpdT-110x8
Jog-1M	Jog-1M	Jog-1M
PM-FK-60mins.	PM-FK-60mins.	PM-FK-30mins.
ST—Maintenance	ST—Maintenance	S&J-220/220x4
		CD-1M
		ST—Maintenance

FRIDAY	FRIDAY	FRIDAY
AM-LSD-3-4M	AM-LSD-2-3M	AM-LSD-2M
PM-Wup-1M	PM-Wup-1M	PM-Wup-1M
REP-1Mx2	REP-880x2	REP-440x3
S&J-220/220x4	S&J-110/110x8	S&J-110/110x8
CD-2M	CD-2M	CD-2M

SATURDAY	SATURDAY	SATURDAY
AM-OFF	AM-OFF	AM-OFF
PM-TT-2M-1½ at full	PM-TT-1M-1320 at full	PM-TT-880-660 at full
speed for time,	speed for time,	speed for time,
stride last 880	stride last 440	stride last 220
INT-440x4	INT-352x4	INT-220x4
S&J-220/220x4	S&J-110/110x8	S&J-110/110x8
TD-30mins.	TD-30mins.	TD-20mins.

SUNDAY	SUNDAY	SUNDAY
RR-12-15M	RR-10-12M	RR-8-10M
ST—Maintenance	ST—Maintenance	ST—Maintenance

AM MILEAGE = 13½	AM MILEAGE = 11½	AM MILEAGE = 9½
PM MILEAGE = 57	PM MILEAGE = 51½	PM MILEAGE = 43
WEEKLY TOTAL = 70½	WEEKLY TOTAL = 63	WEEKLY TOTAL = 52½

MONDAY	MONDAY	MONDAY
AM-LSD-3M	AM-LSD-2M	AM-LSD--2M
PM-Wup-2M	PM-Wup-2M	PM-Wup-2M
SSIT-(1)660x3	SSIT-(1)440x3	SSIT-(1)330x3
(2)660x3	(2)440x3	(2)330x3
(3)440x3	(3)440x3	(3)330x3
(4)440x3	(4)440x3	(4)330x3
CD-2M	CD-2M	CD-2M

TUESDAY	TUESDAY	TUESDAY
AM-TD-20mins.	AM-TD-20mins.	AM-TD-20mins.
PM-FK-4M	PM-FK-3M	PM-FK-2M
S&J-220/220x4	S&J-220/220x4	S&J-165/165x6
SpdT-110x8	SpdT-110x8	SpdT-110x8
CD-1M	CD-1M	CD-1M
ST—Maintenance	ST—Maintenance	ST—Maintenance

WEDNESDAY	WEDNESDAY	WEDNESDAY
AM-OFF	AM-OFF	AM-OFF
PM-Wup-2M	PM-Wup-2M	PM-Wup-2M
REP-880x4	SSIT-(1)660x2	SSIT-(1)440x2
SSIT-(1)440x4	440x2	330x2
(2)352x5	330x2	220x2
S&J-220/220x4	(2)220x2	(2)220x2
CD-2M	330x2	330x2
	440x2	440x2
	S&J-110/110x8	S&J-110/110x8
	CD-2M	CD-2M

THURSDAY	THURSDAY	THURSDAY
AM-Jog-1M	AM-Jog-1M	AM-Jog-1M
SpdT-110x8	SpdT-110x8	SpdT-110x8
Jog-1M	Jog-1M	Jog-1M
PM-TD-60mins.	PM-FK-3M	PM-FK-5M
ST—Maintenance	LSD-3M	ST—Maintenance
	ST—Maintenance	

FRIDAY	FRIDAY	FRIDAY
AM-OFF	AM-OFF	AM-OFF
*PM—Premeet Workout	*PM—Premeet Workout	*PM—Premeet Workout

SATURDAY	SATURDAY	SATURDAY
Competition at 2M	Competition at 1M or 1000 yds.	Competition at 600, 880, or 1000 yds.

SUNDAY—REST	SUNDAY—REST	SUNDAY—REST

AM MILEAGE =8½	AM MILEAGE = 7½	AM MILEAGE = 7½
PM MILEAGE = 40	PM MILEAGE = 34½	PM MILEAGE = 31
WEEKLY TOTAL = 48½	WEEKLY TOTAL = 42	WEEKLY TOTAL = 38½
13 DAY TOTAL = 119	13 DAY TOTAL = 105	13 DAY TOTAL = 91

*Refer to chapter 5, p. 87, "Training the Day Before Competition."

DISTANCE AND MIDDLE-DISTANCE EVENTS
7-DAY TRAINING CYCLE FOR MARCH

*Monday—HARD DAY
*Tuesday—DISTANCE DAY
  Wednesday—HARD DAY
*Thursday—DISTANCE/EASY DAY
*Friday—EASY/LIGHT DAY
  Saturday—COMPETITION/ACHIEVEMENT/HARD DAY
  Sunday—REST/DISTANCE DAY

*AM WORKOUT

SAMPLE TRAINING SCHEDULES FOR MARCH CYCLE

TWO MILE	ONE MILE	880
MONDAY	MONDAY	MONDAY
AM-LSD-3M	AM-LSD-3M	AM-LSD-2M
PM-Wup-1M	PM-Wup-1M	PM-Wup-1M
SSIT-(1)660x4	SSIT-(1)440x4	SSIT-(1)440x4
(2)440x4	(2)440x4	(2)330x4
(3)352x4	(3)220x4	(3)220x4
(4)220x4	(4)110x8	(4)110x4
CD-2M	CD-2M	CD-2M
TUESDAY	TUESDAY	TUESDAY
AM-TD-20mins.	AM-TD-20mins.	AM-TD-20mins.
PM-FK-60mins.	PM-FK-60mins.	PM-FK-45mins.
ST—Maintenance	ST—Maintenance	ST—Maintenance
WEDNESDAY	WEDNESDAY	WEDNESDAY
AM-OFF	AM-OFF	AM-OFF
PM-Wup-2M	PM-Wup-2M	PM-Wup-2M
REP-1Mx2	REP-880x2	REP-660x2
SSIT-(1)440x4	SSIT-(1)352x5	SSIT-(1)330x4
(2)440x4	(2)352x5	(2)330x4
IR-2M	IR-2M	IR-2M
CD-1M	CD-1M	CD-1M

THURSDAY	THURSDAY	THURSDAY
AM-Jog-1M	AM-Jog-1M	AM-Jog-1M
SpdT-110x8	SpdT-110x8	SpdT-110x8
Jog-1M	Jog-1M	Jog-1M
PM-LSD-6M	PM-LSD-5M	PM-LSD-4M
S&J-110/110x8	S&J-220/220x4	S&J-165/165x8
CD-1M	110/110x8	CD-1M
ST—Maintenance	CD-1M	ST—Maintenance
	ST—Maintenance	

FRIDAY	FRIDAY	FRIDAY
(with Saturday	(with Saturday	(with Saturday
Competition)	Competition)	Competition)
AM-OFF	AM-OFF	AM-OFF
PM—Premeet Workout	PM—Premeet Workout	PM—Premeet Workout

FRIDAY	FRIDAY	FRIDAY
(No Saturday	(No Saturday	(No Saturday
Competition)	Competition)	Competition)
AM-LSD-3M	AM-LSD-2M	AM-LSD-2M
PM-Wup-1M	PM-Wup-1M	PM-Wup-1M
REP-880x2	INT-440x4	INT-220x4
440x2	SpdT-110x8	SpdT-110x8
SpdT-110x8	LSD-3M	LSD-2M
LSD-3M		

SATURDAY	SATURDAY	SATURDAY
Competition	Competition	Competition
OR	OR	OR
TT—Back-to-Back	TT—Back-to-Back	TT—Back-to-Back
1½M Trials at	1M Trials at	880 Trials at
7/8 Speed	7/8 Speed	7/8 Speed
OR	OR	OR
SSIT	SSIT	SSIT

SUNDAY	SUNDAY	SUNDAY
REST or RR-10-12M	REST or RR-8-10M	REST or RR-6-8M
ST—Maintenance	ST—Maintenance	ST—Maintenance

AM MILEAGE = 8½-11½	AM MILEAGE = 8½-10½	AM MILEAGE # 7½-9½
PM MILEAGE =41½-53½	PM MILEAGE = 39½-49½	PM MILEAGE = 34½-42½
WEEKLY TOTAL = 50-65	WEEKLY TOTAL = 48-60	WEEKLY TOTAL = 42-52

DISTANCE AND MIDDLE DISTANCE EVENTS
6-DAY TRAINING CYCLE FOR APRIL

```
*Monday—HARD DAY
*Tuesday—DISTANCE DAY
 Wednesday—HARD DAY
*Thursday—EASY DAY
 Friday—LIGHT DAY
 Saturday—COMPETITION DAY
 Sunday—REST

*AM WORKOUT
```

SAMPLE TRAINING SCHEDULES FOR APRIL CYCLE

TWO MILE	ONE MILE	880
MONDAY	MONDAY	MONDAY
AM-LSD-2-4M	AM-LSD-2-3M	AM-LSD-2-3M
PM-Wup-1M	PM-Wup-1M	PM-Wup-1M
REP-1320x4	REP-880x4	REP-660x4
SSIT-(1)220x4	SSIT-(1)220x4	SSIT-(1)220x4
(2)220x4	(2)220x4	(2)220x4
IR-2M	IR-2M	IR-2M
CD-1M	CD-1M	CD-1M
TUESDAY	TUESDAY	TUESDAY
AM-LSD-3M	AM-Jog-1M	AM-Jog-1M
PM-FK-60mins.	SpdT-110x8	SpdT-110x8
ST—Maintenance	Jog-1M	Jog-1M
	PM-FK-60mins.	PM-FK-45mins.
	ST—Maintenance	ST—Maintenance
WEDNESDAY	WEDNESDAY	WEDNESDAY
AM-OFF	AM-OFF	AM-OFF
PM-Wup-2M	PM-Wup-2M	PM-Wup-2M
SSIT-(1)660x4	SSIT-(1)440x4	SSIT-(1)440x4
(2)660x4	(2)440x4	(2)330x4
(3)440x4	(3)440x4	(3)220x4
(4)220x4	(4)110x8	(4)220x4
CD-2M	CD-2M	CD-2M

THURSDAY	THURSDAY	THURSDAY
AM-LSD-3M	AM-LSD-3M	AM-LSD-2M
PM-FK-4M	PM-FK-3M	PM-FK-3M
SpdT-110x12	S&J-220/220x4	S&J-165/165x6
CD-1M	SpdT-110x8	SpdT-110x8
ST—Maintenance	CD-1M	CD-1M
	ST—Maintenance	ST—Maintenance

FRIDAY	FRIDAY	FRIDAY
AM-OFF	AM-OFF	AM-OFF
PM—Premeet Workout	PM—Premeet Workout	PM—Premeet Workout

SATURDAY	SATURDAY	SATURDAY
Competition	Competition	Competition

SUNDAY	SUNDAY	SUNDAY
REST or Loosen Up	REST or Loosen Up	REST or Loosen Up
ST—Maintenance	ST—Maintenance	ST—Maintenance

AM MILEAGE = 10	AM MILEAGE = 8½	AM MILEAGE = 7½
PM MILEAGE = 38½	PM MILEAGE = 36½	PM MILEAGE = 33½
WEEKLY TOTAL = 48½	WEEKLY TOTAL = 45	WEEKLY TOTAL = 41

DISTANCE AND MIDDLE-DISTANCE EVENTS
6-DAY TRAINING CYCLE FOR MAY—EARLY JUNE

    *Monday—DISTANCE DAY
     Tuesday—HARD DAY
    *Wednesday—DISTANCE DAY
    *Thursday—EASY DAY
     Friday—LIGHT DAY
     Saturday—COMPETITION DAY
     Sunday—REST DAY

    *AM WORKOUT

SAMPLE TRAINING SCHEDULES FOR MAY-EARLY JUNE

TWO MILE	ONE MILE	880
MONDAY	MONDAY	MONDAY
AM-FK-3M	AM-FK-3M	AM-FK-2M
PM-LSD-6M	PM-LSD-5M	PM-LSD-4M
S&J-220/220x4	S&J-220/220x4	S&J-165/165x6
CD-1M	CD-1M	CD-1M
ST—Maintenance	ST—Maintenance	ST—Maintenance
TUESDAY	TUESDAY	TUESDAY
AM-OFF	AM-OFF	AM-OFF
PM-TD-20mins.	PM-Wup-1M	PM-Wup-1M
REP-880x2	SSIT-(1)440x4	SSIT-(1)440x4
SSIT-(1)440x4	(2)440x4	(2)330x4
(2)440x4	(3)440x4	(3)220x4
S&J-220/220x4	S&J-110/110x8	IR-2M
CD-1M	CD-2M	CD-1M
WEDNESDAY	WEDNESDAY	WEDNESDAY
AM-Jog-1M	AM-Jog-1M	AM-Jog-1M
SpdT-110x8	SpdT-110x8	SpdT-110x8
Jog-1M	Jog-1M	Jog-1M
PM-FK-60mins.	PM-FK-50mins.	PM-FK-40mins.
ST—Maintenance	ST—Maintenance	ST—Maintenance
THURSDAY	THURSDAY	THURSDAY
AM-LSD-3M	AM-LSD-3M	AM-LSD-2M
PM-Wup-1M	PM-Wup-1M	PM-Wup-1M
S&J-220/220x4	S&J-220/220x4	IR-2M
SpdT-110x8	SpdT-110x8	S&J-110x110x8
IR-2M	IR-2M	SpdT-110x8
CD-1M	CD-1M	CD-1M
FRIDAY	FRIDAY	FRIDAY
AM-OFF	AM-OFF	AM-OFF
PM—Premeet Workout	PM—Premeet Workout	PM—Premeet Workout
SATURDAY	SATURDAY	SATURDAY
Competition	Competition	Competition

SUNDAY	SUNDAY	SUNDAY
REST or Loosen Up	REST or Loosen Up	REST or Loosen Up

AM MILEAGE = 8½	AM MILEAGE = 8½	AM MILEAGE = 6½
PM MILEAGE = 38½	PM MILEAGE =34½	PM MILEAGE = 32½
WEEKLY TOTAL = 47	WEEKLY TOTAL = 43	WEEKLY TOTAL = 39

7 Methods and Techniques for Coaching the Sprint and Hurdle Events

The sprint events in track can be generally defined as races performed with full-speed effort at all times. The hurdle events are in the same category with the addition of the hurdles as obstacles to speed. The events that lie in these categories are the 100, 220, and 440 yard dashes, and the 120 high, 180 low, and 330 or 440 yard intermediate hurdles.

Sprinting and hurdling have become specialty events due to the factors of the start and finish techniques, negotiating hurdles, and running speed. However, in recent years, coaches have realized that sprint athletes need more than natural speed and technique practice in which to succeed in modern-day running.

It is a myth that sprinters cannot endure strenuous training methods. Inherent speed and natural talents have caused some sprint athletes to take workouts lightly. However, there is no substitute for hard work and training on the part of any runner, including sprinters and hurdlers, in reaching his potential and best performance.

TYPES OF SPRINT AND HURDLE ATHLETES

The prime requisites for these events are power, running speed, and motor ability factors such as agility, reaction time, and coordination. The ideal body type for a sprint athlete would be tall, lean and muscular, long legged, and very flexible. The best sprinters and hurdlers usually possess good posture while running. However, since this description does not fit all such runners, we find that sprint and hurdle athletes, just as others, come to us with different qualifications, strengths, and weaknesses. It becomes the coach's job to identify and work with the type of athlete he has. The key to sprinting success is driving power which can be possessed by athletes of all body types.

The Natural, or Inherent, Sprint Athlete

Certain inherent qualities which appear naturally to some runners tend to enhance sprint ability. The so-called natural sprint athlete is superior in such qualities as speed, reaction time, reflex time, educability in motor skills, dominance of right or left movements, and the ability to focus or concentrate attention on the task being performed. Strength, power, and flexibility are also most important, but can be more easily acquired or improved.

The natural sprint athlete is the one most often improperly trained. This type of athlete may also tend to be lazy or inconsistent in training, relying mainly on his natural ability. He will respond best with fast training but needs aerobic running as well, which can be accomplished by the separate use of quality and quantity running. Many natural sprint athletes will regard distance training as punishment work and be negative towards it. However, by properly planned training techniques and separating speed and endurance training, the athlete will better understand the purpose of his program and how it will fulfill his needs and improve performance.

The Power Sprint Athlete

While not possessing as high a degree of inherent motor ability as his more natural counterpart, the power sprinter or hurdler relies on strength and explosive power to make up the difference. His training needs are basically the same as for the natural sprint athlete. That is, the use of separated speed and endurance training. Speed improvement programs as presented in chapter 12 may assist in improving his overall performance.

The Endurance Sprint Athlete

This type of sprint athlete unless possessed with outstanding motor ability qualities will not usually experience as much success in the sprint events as the others. In the hurdle events expertise in technique may make a difference, but he usually will be out-performed by the natural or power sprint athlete. His strength lies in his endurance while sprinting. In other words, the ability to sustain his fastest rate of speed for a longer period of time. He may do better in the longer sprint events and should perhaps stay away from the shorter ones. Speed improvement programs and power strength training can help. Longer distances or increased repetition in quality training will also strengthen him. This type of sprint athlete is the one most likely to participate in cross-country. Without a great deal of natural sprinting ability, the endurance sprint athlete may respond well to the over-distance training method.

RECOGNITION AND SELECTION OF THE SPRINT AND HURDLE ATHLETE

Since running speed is a desired trait in all youngsters, it's never difficult to find the sprint athlete in the school situation. From elementary years on up, these athletes are easily identified by their performance in physical education classes and the desire to demonstrate their speed in athletic situations. However, observation alone is not always reliable since some prospects may have been overlooked or lacked the opportunity to demonstrate their running speed. Screening tests for prospective sprint athletes are quite easy and practical to administer. The best situation in which to give a screening test would be in the physical education class at the end of the eighth grade year or at the beginning of the ninth grade year. By using the physical education class, no student would be overlooked. If the student turned out to be a prospect, it would allow sufficient time to encourage him to participate as well as starting him on a beginning training program.

Screening Test for Sprinters

A. Using a standing start, have the prospect run a 50 yard dash, starting on his own initiative.
B. Start the watch on the first forward movement of the runner.
C. If the prospect completes the run in 6.0 for boys or 7.0 for girls or less, he or she would be considered a potential sprint athlete.

Notes:

1. Have the start and finish line clearly marked.
2. Tell the prospects *not* to stop at the finish line, but to run 10 yards past. A second line for this purpose may help. This will deter the runner from slowing down or pulling up at the finish line, which could greatly influence his time.
3. The screening test does not indicate any real potential for the 440

except that of present running speed. The 440 potential would best be determined after a training program has been in effect.

Screening Test for Hurdlers

A. Set up low hurdles or similar obstacles at the 30 inch height. The course would be 50 yards in length with the hurdles at 15, 25, and 35 yards.
B. Using a standing start, have the prospect run the 50 yard course, starting on his own initiative.
C. If the prospect completes the course in 7.2 for boys or 8.2 for girls or less, he or she would be considered a potential hurdle athlete.

Notes:

1. Use the same procedures as in notes 1 and 2 for the screening test for sprinters.
2. Demonstrate prior to the test the correct way in which to negotiate the hurdles. Let the prospects practice for a short period of time if they so desire. However, do not demand that they clear the hurdle in any one specified way. Let them use whatever they feel is most natural and comfortable at this time.

TRAINING IMPLICATIONS FOR THE SPRINT AND HURDLE EVENTS

At times, the sprint and hurdle events appear to be so specialized that technique work is all that is necessary for good performance. Often the effortless appearance of the athlete while racing is misleading. A vast amount of training is necessary for such performances. There are basically three areas of concentration in training for the sprint and hurdle events. They are distance or aerobic training, anaerobic or speed training, and technique work.

Off-Season Distance Buildup

If not participating in cross-country, a substantial amount of the off-season training should be spent on distance running. The sprint and hurdle events require the same consistency in training as the longer running events. Aerobic training is necessary for recovery in anaerobic events. Cardiovascular and muscular endurance helps the sprinter or hurdler to maintain correct technique and constant speed throughout the race. This is also important in the shorter runs. Regardless of the training method being used, the off-season distance buildup is just as necessary for success in the sprint and hurdle events as in the distance events.

Anaerobic Training

All events up to and including the 440 yard distances are generally regarded as anaerobic events. Anaerobic simply defined means an absence of oxygen or an activity in which oxygen debt will occur. In other words oxygen utilization is not the primary requisite for performance, except for recovery. The sources of energy for anaerobic running are known as the ATP-PC (energy release from the muscles) system and the LA (lactic acid) system. The shorter the event, the more dependence on the anaerobic system. As the events lengthen, the aerobic system becomes increasingly important. Anaerobic training is specific to the task. The specificity of training for the sprint and hurdle events is important to develop the energy systems and the other motor ability factors that are necessary for good performance.

Technique Work

The third training consideration for the sprint and hurdle events is that of technique work. Technique training needs to be combined with anaerobic and aerobic training in proportionate levels to efficiently train the athlete. Technique work should not be a substitute for any other phase of training. Often, especially in hurdlers, the greatest amount of time is spent on technique while other areas of development such as endurance become neglected. By this mode of training, the athlete may be deprived of reaching his maximum potential in performance.

METHODS OF SPRINT AND HURDLE TRAINING

Overdistance Method

The overdistance training method for sprinters and hurdlers is based on a period of preseason distance training and emphasis on overdistance interval and speed work during the other phases of the season. This method may be best utilized by teams not having an indoor season or a year-round program. It advocates that through the overdistance principle the sprint athlete will reach his best performance through increased strength, and muscular and cardiovascular endurance. The disadvantages of the method lie in the possibility of overtraining or physiologically fatiguing the runner and a lack of specificity in training. The endurance type of sprint athlete or a runner in poor condition may benefit most from this method.

Conventional Method

So-called for the lack of a better name, the conventional method is the most popular training method for the sprint athlete. It is based on the full school year excluding a summer program unless the athlete trains and competes on his own. The method offers a balance of aerobic and anaerobic training, placing the emphasis on specificity of training and proportionate quality and quantity running throughout the phases of the season. Bascially the training year is broken down into three phases and consists of the following:

Phase 1—September through December. Cross-country type of distance training—Moderate interval or repetition runs—Hill training—Power strength training.

Phase 2—January to March. Distance runs—Increased interval training—Speed training—Emphasis on quality work—Technique work—Strength training.

Phase 3—March to June. Less distance training—Major emphasis on speed and quality work—Technique work—Strength training—Rest.

Underdistance Method

The underdistance method places little emphasis on aerobic training. Other than for warming up or cooling down purposes, distance runs are seldom used. The main emphasis is on quality running at varied distances and technique work. It is seldom used as a year-round training method unless sufficient rest periods are scheduled. A major disadvantage to the runner is that of peaking too soon or becoming stale. This training has also been referred to as the "speed only" method. The natural sprint athlete may experience more success with this method than others, although it is common to experience "peaks and valleys" from underdistance training. It has been questioned whether this method can increase the potential of the runner or just provide a form of maintenance training.

TECHNIQUES OF SPRINT AND HURDLE TRAINING

Many of the techniques of training sprinters and hurdlers are the same as for the other running events with variations suited to the shorter race distances.

Warming Up

The warming up period for the sprint and hurdle events should be specific and detailed. Slow running or jogging should begin the warm-up session. In early season training, it is recommended that the athletes use the Flexibility Program as presented in chapter 12. This extensive flexibility training will reduce the chance of injury as well as increase flexibility. As the season progresses, the program could be modified. However, the warm-up should not be rushed and the athletes should understand its importance. After the flexibility training, the warm-up can conclude with slightly faster or change of pace running to prepare for the day's training.

Sample Warm-up:

1. Jog 440 to 880 in groups. Stretch legs and bounce lightly during the running.
2. Flexibility training.
3. 440 with three paces—fast, normal, slow. Change pace frequently —accelerate for short bursts.
4. Move on to the day's training schedule.

Distance Training

Fall distance training is best accomplished by the techniques of LSD and timed distance. There should be a slow, progressive build up of the pace and distance to be run. Fartlek is best used once the athlete has built up his endurance from LSD or timed distance. Due to the other training involved, Fartlek is used less in sprint and hurdle training in the off-season. Runs of three to five miles at a pace of under 7 minutes per mile should be the goal of the early season distance buildup. Some successful coaches have used up to 60 minute distance runs during this training period for the sprint athlete.

Hill Training

Hill training during the early season can be very beneficial to building strength. This can be integrated into the distance runs or be a separate part of training. The Uphill Running Speed Improvement Program presented in chapter 12 would be an example of separate hill training. The hill training could be used two to three times weekly depending on the time of the season.

Running Posture

As stated previously, most sprint athletes possess good running posture. Guidelines for sprinting posture are presented in chapter 10. The best time to analyze the sprinter or hurdler's running posture is in the off or early season training when time is available and the athlete can focus his concentration on it. By the time the intense training begins, it would be best if posture were natural to the runner.

Relaxation

Relaxation, while part of running posture, is important enough to be mentioned separately. Relaxation in running must be stressed for the sprint and hurdle athlete at all times. Many coaches will agree that one difference between the quality of sprint athletes is the ability to practice relaxation since it produces more efficient running. Chapters 10 and 12 offer information and techniques for relaxation in running.

Technique Work

The sprint and hurdle events have specialized skills other than running which must be practiced for proficiency. Technique work and drills are introduced into the early season training and progressively become more important as the season moves on. Perfection in execution and performance is the goal of technique work. Some of the most important techniques to be practiced are as follows.

Sprint events—The start, reaction time, acceleration, relaxation, the finish.
Hurdle events—The start, reaction time, negotiating the first hurdle, maintaining stride pattern and acceleration for the remaining hurdles, relaxation, the finish.

Interval Training

The application of interval training to the sprint and hurdle events usually follows two patterns: the use of overdistance or underdistance intervals. This differs from the longer events (880 on up) in which all of the recommended interval distances are under the race distances. The set system of interval training is utilized less, especially in the shorter events. However, it is still an effective technique for 440 training. Interval training in one form or another is generally used throughout the season. The recovery intervals may be longer, but the runs are usually at a faster rate of speed. Variation of the interval distances often makes the training more enjoyable for the runner. The following chart (Table 7-1) illustrates the recommended interval distances and their utilization for the sprint and hurdle events.

TABLE 7-1
INTERVAL TRAINING DISTANCES
FOR THE SPRINT AND HURDLE EVENTS

EVENT	OVERDISTANCE	UNDERDISTANCE	SSIT
100yd Dash 120yd HH	440,330,220, 200,165,150	110,70,55	165,150,110
220yd Dash 180yd LH	660,600,440, 352,330,300	200,165,150, 110	220,165,150, 110
440yd Dash 330 or 440yd IH	660,600,550	400,352,330, 300,220,165, 150,110	352,330,220, 165,110

Speed Training

Commonly referred to as pick up sprints, this type of speed training is a variation of interval training for the sprint and hurdle events. The speed runs are done without as much regard to time. They usually are of short duration, 55 to 110 yards, and are not meant to produce complete fatigue. They are used for anaerobic conditioning often near or at the conclusion of a workout. Examples of this type of speed training would be:

1. Jog 110—sprint 55—walk 55—Repeat as designated.
2. Sprint 55—jog 110—sprint 55—walk 110—Repeat as designated.
3. Sprint 110—walk 110—Repeat as designated.
4. Sprint 110—jog 55—walk 55—Repeat as designated.

Example #2, the sprint, jog, sprint, walk is popular in training because it offers a work bout, partial recovery, another work bout, and recovery.

Acceleration Stride

This is an excellent technique to use in the early season to condition the runner without too much fear of injury. Distances from 55 to about 165 yards can be used. The runner strides the designated distance, constantly accelerating but never reaching full effort, then jogs the same distance and repeats as many times as designated. This is similar to Fartlek based running and helps in teaching and maintaining relaxation. The striding can also be performed by the stride, jog, stride, walk approach if more recovery is necessary.

Pace Starts

Using the sprint start and a stimulus, the runner starts and sprints a designated distance. The purpose is to practice starting technique and full acceleration for a reasonable distance to simulate running conditions. Hurdlers would negotiate the first hurdle just as in their event. 30 to 60 yards are used for short events, while the 440 may go as far as 110 yards.

Finish-Line Sprints

Depending on the event, have the runner jog 50%, stride 25%, and sprint the last 25% of the race distance to the finish line. It is most important to drill the sprint athlete to always finish at his best effort, run relaxed, and not to slow down before crossing the line. Another fault to avoid is the runner turning or glancing to either side as this will considerably slow his forward movement.

Reaction Time

Reaction time is very specific to the task. It is most important upon the start of a sprint or hurdle event. It can be improved through strength, conditioning, the absence of fatigue, and running posture. However due to specificity, the best way a sprint athlete can improve his reaction time is by performing the task (start) under exact conditions. This is why it is imperative that runners have some technique work with the use of the proper commands, time intervals between commands, and the starting gun. Verbal or whistle starts cannot provide quite the same experience or benefits towards improving reaction time.

Speed Improvement Programs

Speed improvement programs for the sprint and hurdle events are best utilized in the fall or early season training. Chapter 12 presents a variety of programs to suit the needs of different athletes.

Strength Training

Chapter 11 presents complete strength training programs for the sprint and hurdle athlete including power training.

Cooling Down

Some type of slower running should conclude the workout. This should not be as extensive as for the middle-distance or distance runner as the training method is different and the cooling down period should not leave the runner fatigued. Usually a 440 to 880 yard run is sufficient unless distance training has been scheduled in which the latter part of the run will serve the purpose. This also is a good time to repeat or use the flexibility training program presented in chapter 12.

All training techniques for the sprint and hurdle events should be used with progression in mind. That is, they should be initiated slow and easy in the off or early season and increased in tempo and intensity as the season progresses.

ANALYSIS OF THE SPRINT EVENTS

100-Yard Dash

    A. START—The type of start used should be suited to the body build of the athlete. Explosive movement out of blocks. Reaction time to stimulus (gun).

B. FIRST 30 YARDS—Rapid acceleration to 90-95% of maximum speed. Body lean forward.
C. 30 TO 60 YARDS—Continued acceleration to maximum (100%) speed.
D. 60 TO 85 YARDS—Steady state of maximum speed. Only can be maintained by relaxed running. Sometimes referred to as "floating" or "coasting."
E. 85 TO 100 YARDS—Some deceleration occurs. This will depend upon the anaerobic condition of the runner. Relaxation is still most important.
F. FINISH LINE—Do not slow down or pull up at tape. *Run completely through (three to four strides) the finish line before slowing down.

220-Yard Dash

A. START TO 60 YARDS—Same as for 100 yard dash.
B. 60 TO 220 YARDS—Steady state or maintenance of maximum speed. This depends highly on the muscular endurance and anaerobic condition of the sprinter. During this coasting or floating phase, it is the ability to maintain maximum speed and run relaxed that indicates the quality sprinter. It has been often stated that it is the runner who slows down the least who will run the fastest time. Obviously some deceleration will occur. The less tension present, the better able the runner to maintain top speed for a longer period of time. Thus, again, the importance of running posture and relaxation!
C. FINISH LINE—Same as for 100 yard dash.
D. CURVE RUNNING IN THE 220—The main principle in running the curve is to stay close to the inside of the lane line. Since a natural tendency exists for the runner to be pulled outward, a slight inward lean is necessary. However, this fluctuates with different lanes. Therefore practice at all lane positions is suggested. A slight lowering of the inside arm and keeping the shoulders at a 90° angle with the curve will help in counterbalancing this pull.

440-Yard Dash

A. START—Same as for 100 yard dash.
B. FIRST 110 YARDS (CURVE)—Gradual acceleration to top speed—No coasting or floating. Relaxation should be present.

---

*There are several techniques at the finish line which are used upon reaching the tape. All are fairly similar and have such names as the "lunge," "jump," "dip," "lean," and "turning the shoulder." However, if a change in body position occurs before the tape is reached, a considerable slowing effect will take place. Therefore the timing of such movements must be perfect and the runner must continue running at full speed through the tape.

C. SECOND 110 YARDS (STRAIGHTAWAY)—Maintenance of maximum speed through relaxation. No deceleration!

D. THIRD 110 YARDS (CURVE)—Use all available muscular power and endurance to maintain maximum speed without tying up. This will depend highly on the strength, muscular endurance, and anaerobic-aerobic condition of the runner. Relaxation must still be present.

E. FOURTH 110 YARDS (STRAIGHTAWAY)—Fatigue will be present! Relaxation, conditioning, running posture, speed maintenance, pain tolerance, and guts will determine the finish of the 440.

F. FINISH—Same as for 100 yard dash.

NOTES ON 440:

1. In most instances, the first 220 will be two to four seconds faster than the second 220. The first 220 should be no more than 2 seconds slower than the runner's best open 220 time. The first 220 must be run fast to produce a good 440 time. Running too far behind or trying to catch up produces more tension and decreases relaxation, especially in the last 110 yards when the lanes even out.

2. There are two predictor formulas which have shown good results in predicting or estimating potential 440 times. The first is best used for a 100-220 sprinter who has not run the 440 on a regular basis. The 100 yard dash time is his best predictor.

FORMULA: Best 100 yard dash time multiplied by 4.4 plus 4.4 seconds.

EXAMPLE: Predicting the 440 potential of a 10.0 100 yard dash. 10.0 x 4.4 = 44.0 + 4.4 = 48.4. This would indicate that with proper training this athlete has the potential to run the 440 yard dash in 48.4.

The second formula is best used to estimate the potential of an athlete already running the 440, and not primarily involved in the short sprints.

FORMULA: Best 220 yard dash time multiplied by 2 plus 4.0 seconds.

EXAMPLE: Estimating the 440 potential of a 22.0 220 yard dash. 22.0 x 2 = 44.0 + 4.0 = 48.0. If the difference between the actual 440 time and the estimated time is more than 1.6 seconds, the runner may not be reaching his full potential in this event.

ANALYSIS OF THE HURDLE EVENTS

120-Yard High Hurdles

A. START—The type of start used should be suited to the body build of the athlete. Explosive movement out of blocks. Reaction time to stimulus (gun). The high hurdler will tend to rise sooner than the sprinter in order to prepare to negotiate the first hurdle.

B. THE FIRST HURDLE—Eight strides and steady acceleration to the first hurdle. Emphasize leading with the knee instead of the foot in lifting and preparing to clear the hurdle. Keeping the shoulders and hips parallel to the hurdle is most important in maintaining acceleration, rhythm, and relaxation in running.

C. THE CONSECUTIVE HURDLES—Upon landing (ninth stride), three strides should be taken between the next nine hurdles. The action is no different than that of the first hurdle. Maintaining the proper stride pattern, speed, and relaxation are key factors. Fatigue effects and deceleration usually begin after the sixth or seventh hurdle. The same principle of coasting or floating also applies here. By anaerobic conditioning and relaxation, the hurdler can maintain a steady state of maximum speed for a longer period of time.

D. THE LAST HURDLE—The final hurdle should be run the same as the previous ones. Before attempting the sprint to the finish line, the last hurdle should be cleared properly. If behind, or if he attempts to rush the last hurdle, the runner will usually break stride, lose relaxation, and finish slower than when using correct technique. If the last hurdle is negotiated properly, the finishing kick should be no different from that of the sprint races.

E. FINISH LINE—The hurdle finish should be exactly the same as described for the sprints including the finish line techniques.

180-Yard Low Hurdles

A. START—Same as for the high hurdles with the exception that the low hurdler may not rise up as quickly due to the five extra yards to the first hurdle.

B. THE FIRST HURDLE—Ten strides and steady acceleration to the first hurdle. Due to the decrease in hurdle height, more emphasis can be placed on accelerating to maximum speed. Relaxation should be maintained.

C. THE CONSECUTIVE HURDLES—Seven strides should be taken between the next seven hurdles. Speed is probably more important than hurdle technique in this race. The maintenance of a steady state of speed and relaxation parallels that of the 220 yard dash.

D. THE LAST HURDLE—Same as for the 120 yard high hurdles.

E. FINISH LINE—Same as for the sprint events.

Note: Many states are replacing the 180 yard low hurdles with the 330 intermediate hurdles as a high school event.

330-440-Yard Intermediate Hurdles

A. START—Same as for the sprint events.
B. THE FIRST HURDLE—21 to 24 strides are used to cover the 49 yard distance to the first hurdle. This depends upon the speed and stride length of the individual runner. The first hurdle is run on a curve and it is important to negotiate it properly as a loss of balance or rhythm here may hamper a good performance in a race. The designation of a certain number of strides is essential and requires considerable time in practice. Rapid acceleration will enable the runner to maintain speed throughout the early part of the race.
C. THE CONSECUTIVE HURDLES—13 or 15 strides between the remaining hurdles are used by most experienced hurdlers. Beginners may feel more comfortable with 17 strides, however it is doubtful if this can produce the best performance. Stride length is the key factor in the number of steps used. Some athletes may use an even number of strides and alternate the lead leg if they can effectively hurdle both ways. Stride maintenance, acceleration, and relaxation are key factors in the early part of the race. A well-conditioned 330 hurdler should not change stride patterns during the run even though many successful 440 hurdlers will increase their steps by 2 in the latter stages of the race. Speed maintenance and the ability to finish strong lies within hurdle technique. Proper technique with as little alteration as possible will limit energy expenditure and control deceleration.
D. THE LAST HURDLE—This is basically the same as for the 120 yard high hurdles, but with an added factor of fatigue. It has been stated that in a close intermediate race, the runner who clears the final hurdle while maintaining speed and relaxation will finish first. This may be of increased importance in the 330 event since the distance from the last hurdle to the finish line is only 12.8 yards as compared to 36.3 yards in the 440 intermediates.
E. FINISH LINE—Same as for the sprint events.

DRILLS FOR THE SPRINT EVENTS

The following drills can add variety and stimulation to the workout as well as offering a means of conditioning and specificity of task for the sprint events.

Indian Run—Same as the technique for cross-country and distance and middle-distance training. However, for sprint events, the track is used and the distance for the Indian Run should not be longer than one mile. It can be used for conditioning purposes or as a means of warming up for faster training.

Handicap Sprints—Two methods of handicapping a sprint run are as follows: (A) Give a one to five yard lead before the start depending on the distance to be run. (B) Have one athlete approach with a running start and as he passes the stationary runner(s), they immediately take off. This type of drill encourages the runner to accelerate rapidly while emphasizing posture and relaxation to catch up when running behind.

Circuit Drill—This may be best used as part of a warm-up or a conditioning drill at the end of a workout. It is a good drill indoors when space is limited. The coach can set up whatever stations he feels will suit the needs of his training program. This can include runs of different lengths and speeds, starts, agility and reaction drills, conditioning exercises, strength training exercises, posture and relaxation running, and finish line techniques. The circuit can be performed at a moderate pace (warm-up) or for a time limit (conditioning).

4-Minute Mile Drill—This drill combines a variety of interval runs which should total four minutes. A time limit can also be given in which to complete the 4 minute mile. Example of combinations are:

- A. 16 x 110 @ 15 seconds.
- B. 8 x 220 @ 30 seconds.
- C. 2 x 440 @ 60 seconds + 8 x 110 @ 15 seconds.
- D. 1 x 440 @ 60 seconds + 1 x 330 @ 45 seconds + 2 x 220 @ 30 seconds + 5 x 110 @ 15 seconds.

Relay Sprints—Run two groups opposite each other using the relay method with one runner going at a time. Use on both curves and straightaways.

Wind Sprints—Group running. Upon coach's signal, the group sprints the designated distance, then walks or jogs back to starting point. Use on both curves and straightaways.

Fast Leg Drill—Four speed running in place.

1. Jogging pace.
2. High knee lift.
3. Sprint hard and low in place.
4. Shake it out.

Repeat as designated or for a time limit.

Short Starts—Runners start themselves and sprint 10-30 yards. Start out easy and then increase to full effort.

Form Running—Concentrate on running posture. Coach can check athlete's posture from front, side, and rear view. Good early season drill to look for posture faults and teach relaxation.

Wave Drill—Reaction and agility. Use on grass. Athletes run in place and change direction upon coach's signal. (Forward, backward, right side, left side).

Rope Skipping—Agility, coordination, and leg strength. Perform various rope skipping skills for a time period. Good indoor early season drill.

Balance Drill—Use board or beam about twelve feet in length, two inches wide, and two feet off the ground. Have runners walk the board, turn, and walk back to help improve balance.

Mountain Climber—A good early season exercise for explosive leg movement and coordination. With the body in a push up position, draw and flex one leg up under the chest. The exercise is performed by alternating the position of the legs (flexed and extended) with an explosive movement for a designated number of repetitions.

DRILLS FOR THE HURDLE EVENTS

The drills presented here can be used both with the beginning and experienced hurdler. It has been stated that most hurdle technique work should be done at a full speed effort, however this is not always possible and the beginner especially will benefit from technique drills at slower speeds. Some drill or technique work should be done occasionally when the athlete is approaching fatigue.

Lead Leg Exercise—Set up a flight of five high hurdles. The athlete runs beside the hurdle using only the lead leg action to step over the hurdle. The practice of the proper arm action should be emphasized. This drill can be done at different rates of speed usually beginning with a slow jog or trot to fully loosen up. The lead leg must be the leg next to the hurdle.

Trail Leg Exercise—This is the opposite or second part of the lead leg exercise. The trail leg is next to the hurdle and the trail leg only negotiates the hurdle using the proper action with the knee pointed straight ahead and the foot everted. Again a flight of five high hurdles is used as well as different rates of speed.

Wall Drill—Use for beginning hurdlers or in correcting form. Place a line across a wall at the desired hurdle height with tape. Start the hurdler by standing still five to six feet from the wall. Kick out and above the line assuming a hurdling position. This drill will aid height and placement in practicing the lead leg action. Once the athlete has accomplished this standing still, have him perform the same drill running in place.

Hurdle Stretch (at high hurdle height)—This is a good exercise to precede any technique work. It consists of three parts. Have the athlete: (A) Place the heel of the lead leg on the top of the hurdle and stretch forward. (B) Turn parallel to the hurdle and place the trail leg across the top of the hurdle (from the knee down). Place the hand on the top of the hurdle for balance and extend the body back and up, rising on the supporting toe. (C) Using the same starting position as (B), bend forward and touch the ground in front of the supporting foot, keeping the knee straight.

One Hurdle Drill—The one hurdle drill is usually used for practicing technique to negotiate the first hurdle. Due to the stride pattern involved, it is best practiced using only that stride pattern. However, some beginners will benefit from just using one hurdle to practice form and technique.

Three Hurdle Drill—This is used to practice stride patterns and technique for consecutive hurdles. The drill may be increased to four or five hurdles on occasion. However the correct stride pattern including the first hurdle should be maintained.

Stamina Drill—Place two flights of five high hurdles on the track next to each other, about five yards apart (Table 7-2). Have the athlete add two steps making his stride pattern now five and run five hurdles down and five hurdles back. Repeat the ten hurdle circuit as many times as designated. It has been stated that when a runner can perform 20 or more circuits without stopping he should be approaching good hurdling condition. Proper form and technique should be emphasized during the drill. If the athlete's technique becomes sloppy, he may be overextending his endurance for that workout.

Box Drill—Triangle Drill—These are two variations of the stamina drill. They are performed in the same manner as the stamina drill. For the box drill, 12 hurdles are set up in a box or square formation and the athlete runs in four directions. The triangle drill consists of 9 hurdles in a triangular shape (Table 7-2). These drills are useful for beginners as observation is easy for instructional purposes. The box and triangle drills offer the coach forward, side and rear views of the hurdler in motion without changing his position. The experienced hurdler can also use them for conditioning purposes.

TABLE 7-2
FORMATIONS FOR STAMINA, BOX, AND TRIANGLE HURDLE DRILLS

STAMINA DRILL	BOX DRILL	TRIANGLE DRILL
X	X X X	X X
X X	X X	X X
X X	X X	X X X /start
X X	X X	X X X
X X	X X X___ start	
X ___ start		

Concentration Drill—Have another athlete run beside the hurdler always staying slightly ahead. By running behind, the hurdler will be forced to accelerate to full speed more quickly, maintain good hurdling technique, and stay in his stride pattern. This drill is best used with a minimum of 5 hurdles and could be used to challenge an exceptional hurdler. The "rabbit runner" should be instructed not to lead by more than about three yards until the final hurdle is cleared. It may become difficult for the hurdler to fully concentrate if the challenge is not realistic.

Taping Stride Patterns—A method especially effective with beginning hurdlers to develop knowledge of the proper stride pattern. It may be used indoors or outside on an all weather track. Use different colored plastic tape for each hurdler and place strips where his stride should land. The hurdler should attempt to land on these markers. This can be done for one hurdle and up to a flight of three. The drill is mainly used for learning and instructional purposes or to aid in correcting faulty stride patterns.

Alternating Lead Leg Drill—This drill is for the intermediate hurdler. It is basically a motor task. The runner using a slow speed practices negotiating each hurdle, leading with his non-dominant leg. An alternation of the lead leg can also be used. Four to six hurdles is sufficient for the drill. While some coaches may not agree with the alternating tactic, the intermediate hurdler may need this skill in an emergency situation. Some experts conclude that similar motor tasks performed with the non-dominant side will improve the motor skill level and performance of the dominant side.

RACE STRATEGY AND TACTICS

Strategy and tactics are rather limited in sprint and hurdle events. Since all these events are run in lanes and are staggered except for the shortest ones, it is not always possible to compete against a visible opponent. In the 440 for example, until the runners reach the final 110 yards, they must run versus time and the track. Planning how to run the event and the goal or time strived for is still important, but offers little flexibility as compared to the longer events. The sprint and hurdle events require full effort. There is no time for a pause or lapse in any race. The most important tactic to success is the proper distribution of speed throughout the race. This combined with mental preparation and motivation will greatly contribute to the overall performance of the well-trained sprint or hurdle athlete.

8

Training Programs for the Sprint and Hurdle Events

PREPARATION FOR COMPETITION

Preparation for sprint and hurdle competition differs somewhat from the longer running events. The strategy and tactics previously discussed make it fairly obvious that there is little margin for error in these events. The athlete should be ready both physically and mentally as race time approaches. It may be easier for the distance runner to be relaxed and loose prior to competition than for the sprint athlete. Preparation for the sprint athlete is more intense as a single pause or lapse in concentration can ruin performance; yet relaxation in performance is still most important. A discussion of the following factors may help the coach in preparing the sprint athlete for competition.

Mental Preparation

The factor of pain tolerance is not as pronounced for the sprint athlete, however mental preparation may be more difficult. The sprint athlete must have confidence in himself and in his ability to win or he seldom will.

The psychological barrier that inhibits ability or causes the athlete to perform below his level is anxiety. Anxiety presents itself as stress, tension, or even fear prior to competition. Anxiety differs from prerace jitters or nervousness by inhibiting performance. In some runners, it may appear as a lack of motivation or even boredom. If the runner cannot overcome anxiety, his performance will be affected.

Almost all athletes experience some type of psychological barrier; however, it is how they react or overcome these barriers that is important. The good runner becomes mentally tough. His emotional state will not turn to anxiety. The emotions can be used to an advantage when pressure develops. Stressful stimuli can improve or decrease performance depending upon the reaction of the individual.

As the coach, you can influence the athlete's mental preparation in many ways. Some suggestions are:

1. If the athlete is physically trained and prepared for competition, chances are he will be less affected by anxiety.
2. Use Psych training methods as discussed in chapter 12 in the overall training of the runner.
3. Do not allow the athletes to compete with each other in practice situations. This may prove self-defeating and create additional barriers.
4. Be aware of the emotional level and needs of different athletes. Use coaching psychology to handle individual differences. If the athlete is highly emotional, a calming or stabilizing influence from the coach may produce the best results. A fearful or an emotionally low-keyed athlete may be best stimulated by arousal tactics such as pep talks and emotional surroundings. Another category, whether we like it or not, is the athlete who responds best to a reward-punishment situation. While this is the least desirable solution, sometimes it is necessary.

Motivation

While some may disagree, motivation in the sprint and hurdle events is usually generated by success. It is seldom that an athlete will maintain genuine interest in these events unless some form of success is taking place. The sprint athlete does not usually have as much intrinsic motivation as the distance runner. This is not to say that he must consistently win or be his team's best, but that he must experience some form of success. Sometimes a relay or jumping event may serve this purpose. Otherwise, the unsuccessful sprinter or hurdler may become discontent and soon leave the track scene. It is very difficult with young sprinters or hurdlers who may mature into top athletes, but become discouraged early in their career. This is the advantage of JV or "B" team competition if such is available. The best remedy that I have found as a coach for such situations is to try to channel the unsuccessful sprint or hurdle athlete into another event that may better suit his abilities. Regardless of success, if the athlete remains motivated and is sincerely interested, the fullest opportunities are extended to him. However, I might add that I have experienced many instances where an average sprinter has developed into a first class 440 or 880 athlete and an average high hurdler has proven a very competitive intermediate hurdler.

Training the Day Before Competition

On the day before competition, the sprint athlete should never run at full speed. Being loose and flexible is important, but the full effort should be saved for the race. Early season or indoor competition necessitates a brief workout the day prior to competition. In the competitive or late season, some coaches may prefer to rest the sprint athlete the day before a race. This needs to be based on the individual runner. If training takes place, a light day is recommended and relaxation in all phases of running should be emphasized. An example of a premeet day workout is as follows.

1. Jog a 440 using the outside lanes of the track.
2. Perform the usual flexibility training and loosening up routine.
*3. Perform acceleration striding at varied speeds in proportion to the race distance.
*4. Practice starts.
*5. Practice finish line techniques.
6. Jog a 440 at a relaxed pace to conclude training.
7. Check out with the coach personally.

*Hurdle technique or drills should be incorporated.

NOTE: Relay practice or drills can be added or incorporated into the workout. This should not be excessive the day prior to a meet (see chapter 9).

Time Trials

Actual time trials will not be of any great benefit if indoor or early season competition is scheduled. The race itself will serve this purpose. Prior to early season competition or if none is planned, achievement runs for evaluation are necessary. This is best accomplished by the use of over-distance trials. Back to back achievement runs at about 3/4 to 7/8 speed are a good method for testing sprint athletes.

There should be little full speed work done during the practice sessions except on specialized techniques. The sprint athlete can peak more quickly than others. Excessive use of full speed efforts or time trials may cause the runner to peak prematurely.

Indoor Competition

The indoor season presents quite a variation for the sprint and hurdle athlete. Indoor races are commonly between 45 and 60 yards. The 440 athlete can participate in the 300, 440, or 600 yard runs. Actually the shorter distances may benefit the sprint athlete. They offer good test distances for full speed efforts while not producing excessive fatigue. The intermediate hurdler may find the 600 yard run most beneficial to his training during the indoor season.

Indoor sprinting and hurdling is most intense. A poor start or one mistake and the runner is out of contention. Indoor running places great emphasis on the start and rapid acceleration during the race. As long as the sprint and hurdle athlete is trained for the outdoor distances, there is no disadvantage to indoor racing.

Running More Than One Event; Trials and Finals; Consecutive Day Competition

The above competitive situations occur more frequently for the sprint athlete. The key factor in all of them is advance preparation. The athlete should be trained for such situations. Physical preparation is most important. This is one of the reasons why the off season training is strongly recommended. The areobic or distance build up will benefit the anaerobic recovery and overall conditioning of the runner.

Mentally, the athlete should be aware of what is expected of him as far as the events he will be participating in and how often he may have to run. The coach should also use his knowledge of the runner and his experience in deciding how many events should be participated in without lowering the level of performance.

Running More Than One Event—The training schedule should offer some practice situations in which the athlete can simulate running multiple events. Back-to-back achievement runs and the set system of interval training are two ways in which this may be accomplished. These need not be full speed efforts as long as they provide the runner with anaerobic work bouts and recovery. Such training should begin during the early season.

Trials and Finals—Anaerobic conditioning is the key factor. Can the athlete perform at full effort, take a rest period, and return to the same or an improved level of performance? One point to mention is that trials should be considered as trials and not finals. If an athlete can still qualify and conserve energy, he should do so. In most trials, two to four people will qualify. The trial should always start and be run at full effort until the runner is assured of his position and what he must do to maintain it. This is not always possible in the shorter events, but neither is it as necessary.

Consecutive Day Competition—This usually occurs only in championship meets. The main factor for the runner is to keep himself mentally ready. He may suffer some letdown if he is used to a hard day-easy day approach to training or resting the day after competition. Practice situations should be planned to prepare for this experience well in advance of the meets. An example would be to schedule a hard training day and then begin the next day's practice with training techniques that will simulate the competition effort. The remainder of the practice then would revert back to the training cycle.

Training the Day After Competition

During the outdoor season when the competition is at its heaviest, it may be beneficial to have the sprint athlete loosen up and do some slow distance training the day following competition. This could be LSD, timed distance, or Fartlek at a distance of 2 to 5 miles.

Rest is most important to the sprint athlete, but should not be overdone. Usually all of the heavy training during the competitive season is done early in the week and tapers off to light training or rest as the meet approaches. After a strenuous race effort, distance training will help the runner recover from fatigue. If the athlete shows up for Monday's workout (normally a hard training day) still feeling the effects of Saturday's race, the practice will not prove very worthwhile. Since Sunday may be scheduled as a rest day with no formal practice, a good suggestion is to inform the runners that it is their responsibility to come to practice on Monday *fully* prepared for a hard training session and not a recovery workout.

THE TRAINING PROGRAM

The training year for the sprint and hurdle events is broken down into three phases: the off-season, the early season, and the competitive season. These phases present the basis for a year-round training program. They are based on one workout per day and designed to allow the runner to reach his top level of performance during the outdoor season. The beginning sprinter or hurdler may require more instruction and technique work with less intensity in the training.

The sprint athlete probably responds best to a strenuous training day followed by a day in which he can recover while still maintaining a sufficient training level. The alternating approach to the training day is followed throughout the program.

Training Phases

The training phases are based on the conventional method which emphasizes progression in the training techniques. By progressing at a slow yet steady rate, the runner is given the best opportunity to reach his maximum potential.

Each training phase has a specific purpose or goal to be accomplished during that time period. They are as follows.

OFF-SEASON (September through December)—A build up of strength, power, muscular and cardiovascular endurance, mainly through the use of distance running, some quality running and strength training.

EARLY SEASON (January to March)—A build up of the anaerobic systems through the use of quality running, limited competition, and emphasis on technique work that is specific to the event.

COMPETITIVE SEASON (March to June)—A balance of training and competition designed to allow the athlete to reach the top level of performance at the desired time(s).

Types of Training Days

The types of training days for the sprint and hurdle events are basically the same as presented for the distance and middle-distance events. However, there is one additional type of training day and some variation in the techniques used. The categories of training days are as follows.

1. *HARD DAY*—Quality running: high intensity work: interval training at varied distances: specialized technique work.

2. *EASY DAY*—Quality running: low intensity work: specialized technique work: varied training techniques.
3. *DISTANCE DAY*—Quantity running: LSD, Fartlek, timed distance: overdistance intervals with low intensity.
4. *FAST DAY*—Speed training: underdistance intervals: varied intensity: specialized technique work.
5. *LIGHT DAY*—Premeet workout: very light training: specialized technique work.
6. *ACHIEVEMENT DAY*—Time trials: achievement runs: pace objectives.
7. *REST DAY*—Complete rest: loosen up: strength train: runner's choice.

NOTE: The training cycles and sample schedules presented are designed for the experienced high school runner. The early season and competitive season training schedules are designed for use following the off-season training program or participation in cross-country. For the inexperienced or novice runner, modifications can be made to adapt the training to his needs and ability level.

KEY TO ABBREVIATIONS FOR THE SPRINT AND HURDLE TRAINING SCHEDULES

AS—Acceleration Striding
*CD—Cooling Down Period
FK—Fartlek
FLS—Finish Line Sprints
FT—Flexibility Training
HT—Hill Training
IR—Indian Run
INT—Interval Training
LSD—Long Slow Distance

PS—Pace Starts
SpdT—Speed Training Techniques
SSIT—Set System of Interval Training
ST—Strength Training
TD—Timed Distance
TT—Time Trial or Achievement Run
TW—Specialized Technique Work or Drills
*Wup—Warm-up

*If the warm-up or cooling down period are not mentioned specifically in the workout, it is assumed that they are automatically contained within the techniques used in that training session.

SPRINT AND HURDLE EVENTS: OFF-SEASON TRAINING

The off-season training program is the same for all sprint and hurdle athletes with the exception of specialized technique work. The training period should begin with the opening of school and continue through the December holiday vacation.

OFF-SEASON TRAINING
5-DAY CYCLE

Monday—DISTANCE DAY
Tuesday—EASY DAY
Wednesday—DISTANCE DAY
Thursday—EASY DAY
Friday—DISTANCE DAY
Saturday—REST
Sunday—REST

SAMPLE TRAINING SCHEDULES FOR OFF-SEASON CYCLE

SEPTEMBER-OCTOBER	NOVEMBER-DECEMBER
MONDAY LSD or TD-2-5M ST-Basic or Power CD-FT	MONDAY LSD-4-7M ST-Power or Specific CD-FT

TUESDAY
Wup-Jog-FT
INT-220 Stride-Walk
   Recovery x 4
HT-400 yds.
CD-1M-FT
	TUESDAY
	Wup-Jog-FT
	TW-Drills
	INT-440x2/330x2/220x2-
	   Stride-Walk Recovery
	HT-700-1000 yds.
	CD-1M-FT

WEDNESDAY LSD or TD-2-5M ST-Basic or Power CD-FT	WEDNESDAY FK-5M ST-Power or Specific CD-FT

THURSDAY
Wup-Jog-FT
INT-330 Stride-Walk
   Recovery x 4
HT-400 yds.
CD-1M-FT
	THURSDAY
	Wup-Jog-FT
	TW-Drills
	INT-440x2/330x2/220x2-
	   • Stride-Walk Recovery
	SpdT-Pick Ups-Spt 55/Jog 110/
	   Spt 55/Walk 110x4
	CD-1M-FT

FRIDAY	FRIDAY
LSD or TD-2-5M	TD-45 mins. Include 500-700
ST-Basic or Power	yds. of HT in the Run.
CD-FT	CD-FT

SATURDAY	SATURDAY
REST	ST-Power or Specific

SUNDAY	SUNDAY
REST	REST

Notes:

End of October Goals:
   LSD/TD—Progress to 5 miles striving for a 7 min. per mile pace or better.
   INT—Start with 4 repetitions and progress to 8. Vary distances at 220-330-440.
   HT—Progress to 1000 yards using whatever length hill available.

SPRINT AND HURDLE EVENTS: EARLY SEASON TRAINING

The early season training formally begins upon return from the December holiday vacation. It will continue until about March depending upon the outdoor schedule. During this training phase, the runner should be trained for the longest event he will be participating in. Separate training schedules should be utilized for different events.

EARLY SEASON TRAINING
6-DAY CYCLE

Monday—HARD DAY
Tuesday—DISTANCE DAY
Wednesday—HARD DAY
Thursday—EASY DAY
Friday—(A) LIGHT (B) LIGHT (C) HARD
Saturday—(A) COMPETITION (B) ACHIEVEMENT (C) DISTANCE
Sunday—REST

SAMPLE TRAINING SCHEDULES FOR EARLY SEASON CYCLE

100-220	120 HH

MONDAY
Wup-Jog-FT
TW-Starts-Drills
INT-330x4
   150x4
SpdT-Pick Ups-Spt 110/Jog 55/
  Walk 55x4
CD-880-FT
	MONDAY
	Wup-Jog-FT
	TW-1 Hurdle Drill-Stamina
	  Drill-10 Circuits
	INT-220x4
	AS-110/110x8
	CD-880-FT

TUESDAY LSD-5M with some HT ST-Specific or Maintenance CD-FT	**TUESDAY** LSD-5M with some HT TW-3 Hurdle Drill ST-Specific or Maintenance CD-FT

WEDNESDAY
Wup-Jog-FT-Drills
PS-50 yds x 6
SSIT-(1)165x4
    (2)165x4
AS-110/110x8
LSD-2M
CD-FT
	WEDNESDAY
	Wup-Jog-FT-Drills
	PS-1 Hurdle Drill + 35yds x 6
	SSIT-(1)165x4
	    (2)165x4
	TW-Box or Stamina Drill-
	  Maximum Number of Circuits
	  for Present Condition
	CD-880-FT

THURSDAY Wup-Jog-FT TW-Starts IR-1M AS-220/220x4 FLS-55yds x 4 CD-880-FT ST-Specific or Maintenance	**THURSDAY** Wup-Jog-FT TW-Light Drills-Starts IR-1M AS-220/220x4 FLS-30yds x 6 with Last Hurdle CD-880-FT ST-Specific or Maintenance
FRIDAY A. Premeet Workout B. Premeet Workout-TW C. TW-INT-SpdT-AS	**FRIDAY** A. Premeet Workout B. Premeet Workout-TW C. TW-INT-SpdT-AS
SATURDAY A. Competition B. TT-Achievement Run C. FK-ST	**SATURDAY** A. Competition B. TT-Achievement Run C. FK-ST

SUNDAY	SUNDAY
REST	REST

440	180 LH-330 and 440 IH

MONDAY	MONDAY
Wup-Jog-FT	Wup-Jog-FT
TW-Starts	TW-Starts-1 Hurdle Drill-3
INT-660x4	Hurdle Drill
330x4	INT-660x4
AS-220/220x4	330x4
LSD-2M	AS-220/220x4
CD-FT	LSD-2M
	CD-FT

TUESDAY	TUESDAY
LSD-5M with some HT	LSD-5M with some HT
ST-Specific or Maintenance	TW-3 Hurdle Drill
CD-FT	ST-Specific or Maintenance
	CD-FT

WEDNESDAY	WEDNESDAY
Wup-Jog-FT	Wup-Jog-FT
PS-110x6	PS-1 Hurdle Drill+50yds x 6
SSIT-(1)352x4	SSIT-(1)352x4
(2)352x4	(2)352x4
AS-220/220x4	TW-3 Hurdle Drill-Alternating
LSD-2M	Lead Leg Drill
CD-FT	LSD-2M
	CD-FT

THURSDAY	THURSDAY
Wup-Jog-FT	Wup-Jog-FT-Light Drills
TW-Starts	TW-Stamina Drill-10 Circuits
IR-1M	IR-1M
SpdT-Pick Ups-Spt 110/Jog 110/	FLS-110x4 with Last Hurdle
Spt 110/Walk 110x4	CD-880-ST
FLS-110x4	ST-Specific or Maintenance
CD-880-FT	
ST-Specific or Maintenance	

FRIDAY	FRIDAY
A. Premeet Workout	A. Premeet Workout
B. Premeet Workout-TW	B. Premeet Workout-TW
C. TW-SSIT-AS	C. TW-SSIT-AS

SATURDAY	SATURDAY
A. Competition	A. Competition
B. TT-Achievement Run	B. TT-Achievement Run
C. FK-ST	C. FK-ST

SUNDAY	SUNDAY
REST	REST

SPRINT AND HURDLE EVENTS: COMPETITIVE SEASON TRAINING

The competitive season training phase should begin approximately two weeks prior to the major portion of the outdoor season and continue until its completion in May or June. This training phase is designed to prepare for weekly competition.

COMPETITIVE SEASON TRAINING
6-DAY CYCLE

Monday—HARD DAY
Tuesday—FAST DAY
Wednesday—HARD DAY
Thursday—EASY DAY
Friday—LIGHT OR REST DAY
Saturday—COMPETITION
Sunday—REST OR DISTANCE DAY

SAMPLE TRAINING SCHEDULES FOR COMPETITIVE SEASON CYCLE

100-220	120 HH
MONDAY	MONDAY
Wup-Jog-FT	Wup-Jog-FT
TW-Starts and Drills	TW-1 Hurdle Drill
SSIT-(1)165x4	SSIT-(1)165x4
(2)150x4	(2)150x4
(3)110x4	(3)110x4
AS-220/220x4	TW-Stamina Drill-5 to 10 Circuits
LSD-2M	LSD-2M
CD-FT	CD-FT

TUESDAY	TUESDAY
Wup-Jog-FT	Wup-Jog-FT
PS-40yds x 10	PS-1 Hurdle Drill+25 yds x 10
SpdT-Pick Ups-Spt 55/Jog 110/	SpdT-Pick Ups-Spt 55/Jog 110/
Spt 55/Walk 110x8	Spt 55/Walk 110x8
FLS-55yds x 6	FLS-60yds x 6 with Last Hurdle
CD-880-FT	CD-880-FT
ST-Maintenance	ST-Maintenance

WEDNESDAY	WEDNESDAY
Wup-Jog-FT	Wup-Jog-FT
TW-Starts	TW-Light Drills
INT-440x2	INT-440x2
330x2	7 Hurdles x 4
IR-1M	IR-1M
AS-220/220x4	AS-220/220x4
LSD-2M	LSD-2M
CD-FT	CD-FT

THURSDAY	THURSDAY
Wup-Jog-FT	Wup-Jog-FT
TW-Starts	TW-Light Drills
PS-60yds x 6	PS-1 Hurdle Drill+35yds x 6
SpdT-Pick Ups-Spt 110/Jog 55/	TW-Full Flight (10 Hurdles) x 2
Walk 55x4	1. First 5 Stride Pattern-
AS-110/110x4	Last 5 ½ speed
CD-880-FT	2. First 5 ½ speed - Last 5
ST-Maintenance	Stride Pattern
	SpdT-Pick Ups-Spt 110/Jog 55/
	Walk 55x4
	CD-880-FT
	ST-Maintenance

FRIDAY	FRIDAY
Premeet Workout or REST	Premeet Workout or REST

SATURDAY	SATURDAY
Competition	Competition

SUNDAY	SUNDAY
REST or LSD-ST	REST or LSD-ST

440	180 LH-330 and 440 IH
MONDAY	**MONDAY**
Wup-Jog-FT	Wup-Jog-FT
TW-Starts	TW-1 Hurdle Drill
SSIT-(1)352x4	SSIT-(1)352x4
(2)330x4	(2)330x4
(3)220x4	(3)220x4
AS-220/220x4	TW-3 Hurdle Drill
LSD-2M	LSD-2M
CD-FT	CD-FT
TUESDAY	**TUESDAY**
Wup-Jog-FT	Wup-Jog-FT
PS-110 yds x 6	PS-1 Hurdle Drill+60 yds x 6
SpdT-Pick Ups-Spt 110/Jog 55/ Walk 55x8	SpdT-Pick Ups-Spt 110/Jog 55/ Walk 55x8
FLS-110 yds x 6	FLS-110 yds x 6 with Last Hurdle
AS-220/220x4	TW-Stamina Drill-10 Circuits
CD-880-FT	CD-880-FT
ST-Maintenance	ST-Maintenance
WEDNESDAY	**WEDNESDAY**
Wup-Jog-FT	Wup-Jog-FT
TW-Starts	TW-Light Drills
INT-660x2	INT-660x2
500x2	5 Hurdles x 4
400x2	IR-1M
IR-1M	AS-220/220x4
AS-220/220x4	LSD-2M
LSD-2M	CD-FT
CD-FT	
THURSDAY	**THURSDAY**
Wup-Jog-FT	Wup-Jog-FT
PS-110 yds x 6	PS-1 Hurdle Drill+60 yds x 6
SpdT-Pick Ups-Spt 110/ Walk 110x8	TW-Full Flight (10 Hurdles) x 2
AS-220/220x4	1. First 5 Stride Pattern- Last 5 ½ speed
CD-880-FT	2. First 5 ½ speed-Last 5 Stride Pattern
ST-Maintenance	SpdT-Pick Ups-Spt 110/Walk 110x8
	CD-880-FT
	ST-Maintenance
FRIDAY	**FRIDAY**
Premeet Workout or REST	Premeet Workout or REST

SATURDAY Competition	**SATURDAY** Competition
SUNDAY **REST** or LSD-ST	**SUNDAY** **REST** or LSD-ST

9 How to Organize and Coach the Relay Events

THE BASICS OF RELAY RUNNING

Relay events are a popular and exciting part of American track since they not only offer spirited competition, but can provide the difference between winning and losing a meet. A quick analysis of the results will show the effects that relays have had upon the outcome of the meets. With these events and their point values at stake, it is well worth the time and effort necessary to train the relay teams properly. Relay success begins with the coach.

A coach must develop a definite plan for relays. This should include the type of baton pass to be used, how the runners will be selected, how they will be positioned in the race, the amount of practice time to be spent, motivational factors, and development of a positive attitude toward relays. A knowledge of the rules is also important. In order to teach the athletes properly, the coach should know and understand all phases of the rules governing zones, passing the baton, penalties, etc.

The attitude of the coach toward relays and the amount of time and interest shown in their practice will help develop interest on the part of the athletes. How many times have you witnessed the following? Superior runners defeated by poor baton passing or timing; a team trying to learn passes prior to the race; a coach trying to round up four men to enter the event; a team not giving its best because some members don't want to run or because the meet is already decided. These situations will occur less frequently if the coach possesses a positive attitude and is able to instill it in his runners.

PRIDE AND MOTIVATION

The easiest way to develop pride and motivate runners is to win. Nothing succeeds like success. During one outdoor season four of our dual meets went down to the final event, the mile relay. We were successful in all four attempts. Over a three-season period the same mile relay team won 30 consecutive dual meets plus five championship meets in their event. It was not difficult to instill pride or motivate these athletes. In addition, our 440 relay team, while not experiencing the same success, was no less motivated or lacking in pride. It was an honor to be selected for either team. Generally, success is not instant; therefore, it may take time to build or develop a relay team. Some other motivating factors are as follows:

1. Develop a sense of team pride. Let the runners know how important a part they play in the team score. Winning or losing a meet can rest on their performance.
2. Develop a sense of relay team pride. Being a part of the relay team should be an honor. All four runners are dependent upon the performance of their teammates. No one person can win alone; it must be a combined effort. Loyalty and comradeship are important.
3. Competition for selection. Let the selection of the relay team be a competitive situation. Be fair and give all interested runners an equal opportunity to make a team.
4. Conditioning. As is true in any event, an athlete is more confident and will give a higher level of performance when in top condition. Make sure each relay team member is conditioned for the relay event especially if it is longer than his regular events. A conditioned athlete can also work harder for perfection.
5. Practice. It is important that all relay runners practice at the same time and all do the same relay drills, exercises or workouts together. Practicing this way will add to their performance as well as develop team spirit and pride.

SELECTION OF RELAY RUNNERS

The most important characteristic of a relay runner is to be a competitive athlete. No matter what distance must be made up or how close the race is, the competitor is going to run to win. This trait should not belong just to the anchor leg, but to all four runners. A competitive relay runner will achieve the best times when competition forces him to do so, and more often than not will win. Selecting runners is not always an easy task. Certain characteristics make some athletes more desirable for relays than others.

Give all interested candidates an opportunity to make the team. They should train for their own events plus the relay training. All are taught and practice baton passes, drills, etc. Then six runners are selected for each event based on their achievements in practice and competitive situations. This is done so that there will be well-trained reserves in case of injury, illness or other unforeseen circumstances. By having extra men prepared to step in, morale is not lost, efficiency is not hampered, and success is more likely. Also, this procedure discourages a lax attitude from developing in the runners because they know they can be replaced and must work hard to hold the position. If a runner is to be replaced for a reason other than injury, it is usually based on meet performances where he has not performed up to his ability. When selection is difficult or the performances of the runners are close, select mainly on the basis of experience and who is the most competitive runner.

Other factors which should be considered in selection are:

1. The athlete's ability to respond to coaching.
2. The team man over the loner type.
3. Consistency of the athlete.
4. The mental toughness he possesses.
5. Ability to handle baton passes.
6. The athlete who is relaxed under pressure.
7. The athlete who is willing to put in extra time.
8. Desire for success.

Some negative factors to note and avoid are:

1. Avoid undependable and inconsistent athletes.
2. Avoid hypochondriacs.
3. Avoid quitters.
4. Avoid athletes who cut practice.
5. Avoid chronic complainers, gripers, and know-it-all types.
6. Avoid athletes who will not push themselves.
7. Avoid athletes with irregular or odd behavior.

These types of individuals can be detrimental to the success of a relay program.

POSITIONING OF RELAY RUNNERS

Positioning runners for a relay depends mainly on three factors: 1) speed, 2) ability to pass and receive the baton, and 3) the type of runner the athlete is. Coaches should consider these factors in choosing positions, but should also lean heavily on knowledge of their own athletes. There are many theories today regarding which athlete should run first, second, etc. However, it should be stated that whatever theory a coach believes in should work. Otherwise, he should look into other possibilities which might better suit his personnel.

When selecting the proper runners for each leg, use two criteria. The first is speed and the second is a combination of passing ability and the type of runner. Try to fit the athlete into the position that suits him best. Neither criterion has priority and many times, trial and error on the practice field or experience in actual competition influences the final decision.

Position for Sprint Relays Based on Speed

First Leg—second fastest runner.
Second Leg—slowest runner.
Third Leg—third fastest runner.
Fourth Leg—fastest runner.

Position for Sprint Relays Based on Other Factors

First Leg—Best starter from the blocks—a curve runner with the ability to get the lead. He should be the second best competitor. A late pass may enable him to run further distance.

Second Leg—Best baton man—the first pass is important because an early mistake can cost the race. A runner is able to run more relaxed if he has the lead.

Third Leg—Second best baton man—a curve runner who is able to run well under pressure, hold the lead or catch up. He must have a good pass with the anchor leg.

Fourth Leg—Best competitor—a runner who is able to fight off competition or make up yardage—a winner. An early pass can enable him to run further distance.

Position for Distance Relays Based on Speed (Mile Relay and Up)

First Leg—third fastest runner.
Second Leg—second fastest runner.
Third Leg—slowest runner.
Fourth Leg—fastest runner.

Position for Distance Relays Based on Other Factors

First Leg—Best baton man—he could be in a crowd, so the first pass is crucial. He should be able to get the lead or stay near the front, be a quick starter, and the best lane runner.

Second Leg—Speed runner—a free runner and sprint-for-the-lead type. He should be able to get the lead, open up a margin, and be a good baton man in or out of a crowd.

Third Leg—Second best competitor—he must hold the lead or stay within distance to win. He should be a team man, finish strong, and make a good pass to the anchor leg.

Fourth Leg—Best competitor—have a desire to win at all costs. He should be a strong runner, have a good mental attitude, and run best under pressure.

COACHING THE RELAY START

For any relay start that is less than 880 yards, the runner should use a sprinter's start with starting blocks. The accompanying illustrations show five methods of grasping the baton during the sprint start.

As shown in illustration 9-1, the pinch grip on the baton enables the runner to keep his hand in the normal starting position. This grip does not offer the best baton security, because the baton is not fully grasped until after the start.

The three-finger grip (illustration 9-2) offers good baton security; however, it lays the three rear fingers on the track. During the start, the thumb and forefinger support the body weight. Some athletes will feel off-balance using this grip.

Many athletes find the one-finger grip awkward and uncomfortable (illustration 9-3). It does enable the runner to distribute his body weight evenly upon his hand, but does not give the most secure grip on the baton.

The two-finger grip allows the runner to distribute the body weight equally upon his thumb, forefinger, and little finger (illustration 9-4). It offers a secure grip and keeps the baton higher off the track. Most athletes find this method comfortable and natural to the sprint start.

Illustration 9-5 shows a grip which eliminates the use of the forefinger for support in starting. This can cause balance problems. The position of the hand is similar to that of the pinch grip.

Use of the two-finger grip (illustration 9-4) is recommended because

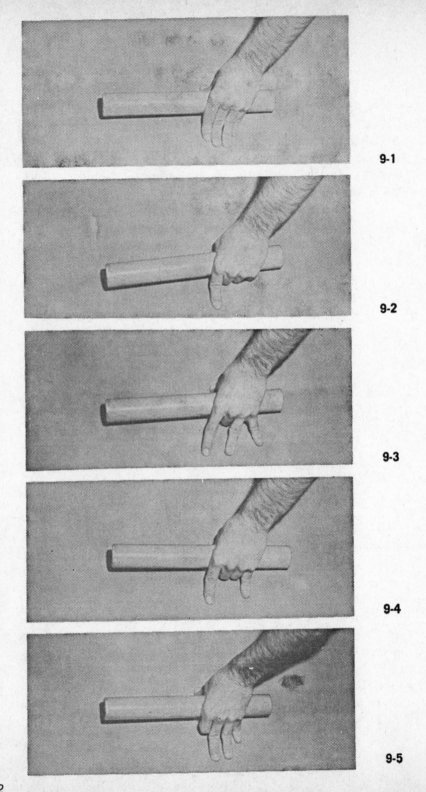

9-1

9-2

9-3

9-4

9-5

it distributes the body weight more equally upon the hand and offers adequate baton security. Most athletes find it more comfortable than the other methods. All of these methods have been used successfully to some extent. The athlete's preference or the coach's philosophy is the deciding factor.

For a standing or non-staggered start in runs longer than 880 yards, the baton should be held in front of the body (illustration 9-6) in order not to have it knocked away or dropped upon the start. Jockeying for position and flying elbows are common causes of losing hold of the baton.

A small amount of time is all that need be spent on the lead-off runner's grasp. If, even once, a runner is prevented from taking off without the baton, dropping it after he starts, or having it knocked away, the time has been well spent.

9-6

PASSING THE BATON

The baton pass, sometimes referred to as the EQUALIZER, is the most important technique in relay racing. All track coaches want their fastest men in each event; however, it is not uncommon to see a team with superior speed defeated. Usually the loss is due to the pass. The method and perfection of the pass is a must for success.

There is no one method of passing. In fact, there are three accepted methods each for sprint relays and distance relays. The selection of the method of passing for a team should be based on sound concepts. The following criteria should be considered:

1. Which method fits the ability level of the athletes.
2. Which method gives the most efficiency in performance.
3. Which method is best for running posture.
4. Which method enables the runners to stay at maximum speed for the longest period of time.
5. Which method will allow free distance to be gained.
6. Which method provides a greater amount of simplicity.

Of the above, the first five are based on performance factors. Simplicity defined for this purpose means certainty in execution, or KEEP THE PASS AS SIMPLE AS POSSIBLE. The relay runners should be confident that they can execute the pass with a minimum of error.

The passes described here are not revolutionary. They are the result of efforts to try to find the methods that can be performed best with fewest mistakes. The results are a combination of various methods into one pass.

There are five common mistakes. Every relay runner must try hard:

1. Not to drop the baton during the pass.
2. Not to leave the passing zone before completion.
3. Not to have a "messy" pass.
4. Not to have the receiver slow down for the pass.
5. Not to have either man alter his running posture prior to the pass.

The point is this: If our athletes make fewer mistakes than the opponents, even if the opponents are faster, the team can win. Thus, each runner has more confidence in himself and the team.

Sprint Relay Pass

The receiver uses a standing take-off taking maximum advantage of the ten-meter (11-yard) zone designated by the International Rule of 1962. He should crouch slightly forward as if he were in a standing SET position, looking back through his left shoulder for the passer. He should not sway or waver upon the take-off. He should keep position against the lane line opposite his receiving arm.

At a predetermined point, the receiver takes off and begins to accelerate toward his maximum speed. As shown in Illustration 9-7, the passer is running at top speed and moving faster than the receiver.

With his built-up speed over the sprint distance (Illustration 9-8), the passer has now cut down the interval between himself and the receiver, who is still accelerating.

The receiver (Illustration 9-9), still accelerating, is nearing the middle of the passing zone, while the passer has continued to cut down the distance between them. Neither man has slowed down.

The actual pass begins as the passer gives the command DOWN, which signals the receiver to begin his BREAK position to receive the baton. The pass takes place quickly as the receiver breaks at the waist and extends his arm, palm up, to receive (Illustration 9-10). Notice the passer is still running at top speed with good posture and extends himself and the baton so that he is able to get as much free distance as possible.

Illustration 9-11 shows the pass being completed. Only the front one-third of the baton is given. The pass is made completely parallel to the ground. The arms of both runners are in a direct line with each other.

In Illustration 9-10, notice that the receiver's arm is straight and his palm is up and flat. Notice in Illustration 9-11 that the receiver is bent at the waist; however, his back is straight and his head is held erect to maintain form and balance. The passer extends the baton with a quick forward-downward motion. He is looking the baton into the receiver's hand. Both runners still have good posture.

The pass being completed, the receiver brings the baton forward and continues to accelerate to maximum speed (Illustration 9-12). He has maintained his stride and posture, and carrying the baton has not caused any alterations. There were no pauses or dead spots where either runner had to slow down or alter his stride.

Coaching Points for the Sprint Relay Pass

1. At all times during the pass, concentrate on running posture.
2. The baton does not change hands at any time during the race. Alternate the pass. A pass made on the straightaway is best executed right to left. A pass made on the curve is best executed left to right. This procedure will keep the runners closer to the inside lane line and cut down the distance on the curves.

9-7

9-8

9-9

9-10

9-11

9-12

9-13

9-14

9-15

9-16

9-17

9-18

3. The receiver's point of take-off will vary in different runners. Usually, the distance is between 8 and 12 yards. Maintaining proper distance should be emphasized because poor judgment on the take-off can destroy the pass.

4. The receiver should position himself so that the passer's arm and his receiving arm are in a direct line with each other. There should be no angles in the pass.

5. The command DOWN should be given only when the pass is to be made. The actual passing time is fast. An early or late command can upset the timing considerably. The word DOWN is used because it tells the runners what to do and is easily pronounced, which can cause less confusion in a race. Any sharp verbal command should serve basically the same purpose.

6. The best position for the pass is to have both runners as far apart as possible in order to gain free distance. A team should never run more than the race distance and by picking up free distance on the pass and running closer to the inside lane line, they can actually run less than the set race distance.

7. The pass should be completed with about 2 to 4 yards remaining in the zone.

8. The break position for the receiver should be:
    A. A definite break at the waist, but keep the back straight and the head up.
    B. The extended arm should be held tightly to the body.
    C. The extended palm is up and flat with the thumb pointing to the rear.
    D. Do not move the extended arm.
    E. Upon receiving, the arm and pass should be parallel to the ground.
    F. After receiving the baton, bring the arm forward quickly and continue running at full speed.

9. After the signal DOWN and the receiver breaks, the passer should:
    A. Extend the baton, but not reach with it.
    B. Pass the baton with a quick, sharp downward and forward motion.
    C. Place only the front one-third of the baton in the receiver's palm.
    D. Complete the pass within 3 or 4 yards.
    E. The pass should be completed with both runners as far apart as possible.

10. The passer is responsible for the success of this pass.

The following may seem elementary, but can be effective as a checklist for each runner, and is easy to memorize.

TEN COMMANDMENTS FOR THE SPRINT RELAY PASS

PASSER:

1. I will concentrate on my running posture.
2. I will give the command DOWN when the pass is ready to be made.
3. I will complete the pass as far apart as possible.
4. I will not slow down when I pass.
5. I will pass the baton quickly.
6. I will use a sharp down and forward movement when I pass.
7. I will give only the front third of the baton.
8. I will not reach with the baton.
9. I will complete the pass in 3 to 4 yards.
10. I am responsible for the success of this pass.

RECEIVER:

1. I will set my take-off mark accurately.
2. I will take off when the passer reaches the mark.
3. I will take off without swaying.
4. I will accelerate to full speed.
5. I will break upon the command DOWN.
6. I will keep my back straight and my head up.
7. I will keep my extended arm into my body.
8. I will keep my extended palm up and flat.
9. I will not move my arm until the pass is received.
10. After I receive the baton, I will run.

Distance Relay Pass

As shown in Illustration 9-13, the receiver uses a standing take-off. He should be turned sideways toward the inside of the track. From this position he can best observe the incoming runner and his position. The receiver's actual take-off is not as fast as it is for the sprint relay.

When the passer has reached the predetermined mark (Illustration 9-14), the receiver takes off at a medium stride in order not to outrun the passer. Both men should concentrate on their running posture.

Approaching the middle of the zone, the passer calls GO, the receiver turns, extends his left arm back, palm up, thumb pointing to the rear, and prepares to accept the baton. The receiver's arm must be kept straight and steady (Illustration 9-15).

As shown in Illustration 9-16, the passer extends the baton into the receiver's open palm with a quick forward motion. The receiver will literally take the baton away. Notice how the receiver is looking the baton into his hand. The passer should not extend the baton until he is in reach of the receiver. Overreaching, especially when fatigued, may cause the passer to lose his balance or even fall before completing the pass.

The receiver has taken the baton and is preparing to turn and accelerate (Illustration 9-17). Notice the balance, leg and arm position of the receiver. The pass is completed just past the middle of the zone.

Illustration 9-18 shows the receiver has turned, brought the baton forward, and is rapidly approaching full stride.

Coaching Points for the Distance Relay Pass

1. The baton does change hands. The pass is made right to left. Thus, the receiver is able to turn toward the inside of the track, his left side. From this position he can lean or move to the inside lane faster and he has a full view of that area.
2. The predetermined take-off mark is usually 2 to 3 yards outside of the zone.
3. GO is used as the verbal command mainly to differentiate from the sprint relay and its different execution. Again, any sharp verbal command, even calling the runner by name, could accomplish the same task.
4. The pass should be completed past the mid-line of the zone. By so doing, it is possible to stay out of the crowd during the pass.
5. The receiver is responsible for the completion of this pass. Due to the fatigue factor of the longer runs (440 and over), the passer will not have as much left at the end of his run. This is the main reason why the receiver is responsible because he will be able to judge his speed and control of the pass. There should be no dead spots during the pass.
6. Points to emphasize for the passer:
    A. He must finish as strong as possible.
    B. He must concentrate on his running posture.
    C. Give the verbal signal GO when the pass can be made comfortably.
    D. Extend the baton only when the pass is to be made.
    E. Extend the baton quickly to the receiver. Do not reach out and try to catch up with an extended baton.
7. Points to emphasize for the receiver:
    A. He must not outrun the passer.
    B. On the GO signal, turn quickly and extend the left arm back, palm up, offering a still target for the passer.

    C. Once the baton is extended, the receiver should take it quickly.

    D. He should look the baton into his hand.

    E. After taking the baton, turn quickly and accelerate.

8. While the sprint relay pass is more complex in its execution, the distance relay pass should not be taken lightly. There is just as much of a need for the distance pass to be practiced under competitive conditions.

Fatigue, which will be present in the passer, cannot be ignored. Runners using half-speed to feign fatigue can practice fundamentals, but their reactions are not the same as when they are in competition. Therefore, some practice must take place under extreme fatigue conditions so that the runners can relate to the competitive situation.

PRACTICING FOR THE RELAYS

Relay practice should be an integral part of the practice schedule from the beginning of the season. Time spent early on the relays will develop more skill in the technique and baton passes. These sessions will save time later in the season as well as increase the efficiency of early season performance. The relay runners must be ready when the competitive season starts.

Off Season (September-October-November)

If the athlete is participating in cross-country, this is sufficient preparation for the relays. For those athletes not engaged in another activity, the time should be spent on building endurance and strength. The off-season program for sprinters, including strength training, should be followed at this time.

Preseason (December-January)

Each athlete should follow the regular workout designated for each event. In addition, three times weekly, 30 to 40 minutes of relay practice should be scheduled before or after the workouts for all interested candidates. These three sessions are spent mainly on theory, technique, and passing. Drills make up the main part of this practice. The coach should conduct and supervise the activity at all times. On the other days, 20 to 30 minutes should be spent by each prospective relay candidate on the drills. From these sessions, observations, time trials, and practice meets, if any, the process of selecting the six runners for each relay event is started.

Early or Indoor Season (February-March)

Again regular workouts are followed and relay practice is added before or after their completion. All six runners are involved, and even though tentatively a first team is selected, the substitute runners will trade off at all positions so they can fill any situation that may occur. At least 20 to 30 minutes per day should be spent on drills and the smoothing out of any trouble spots that may be occurring. The positioning of the runners for each relay should be worked out prior to any competition.

Depending upon what part of the country you are situated in, indoor or outdoor competition will be taking place. While the relay times may not equal later performances, any competition at this time is valuable to gain experience and evaluate personnel.

Outdoor Season (April-May-June)

At this time, it is not expected that critical mistakes will be made due to the lack of technique or practice. Therefore, most of the relay work will be spent on perfecting the baton pass under competitive conditions. The amount of time spent on relays will be dictated by the meet schedule. If possible, some part of each practice should be devoted to the relays. Occasionally, an entire practice can be spent on relays for the runners involved. This is best for a day following competition or early in the practice week. Using the day prior to a meet for extended workouts on relays is not recommended.

DRILLS FOR RELAYS

1. Baton Running—Have each runner carry a baton while doing distance work or during the regular workouts. By practicing this, carrying the baton will become more natural to running posture.

2. Lap Drill—While running laps on the track, a pass is initiated for every 110 yards. The four men run in single file, and using proper technique, pass the baton until it reaches the lead runner. He then lets the other three men go by and resumes the passing.

3. Still Passing Drill—The four runners line up standing still within passing range of each other. The baton is then passed forward quickly by command until it reaches the lead man. The runners then reverse direction and resume passing. This drill is mainly used to check passing and receiving positions.

4. Single Pass Exercise—Break up into groups of two and have each man pass to the other, observing the passing zone. Reverse the direction to save time. This is a good drill for teaching purposes and supervising large groups.

5. Three-Man Drill—This is basically the same as the single pass exercise except that there are three runners to a group. Each man will alternate into the drill. The third man can help in correcting errors and establishing take-off points, etc. This requires less supervision from the coach.

6. Full-Speed Drill—This drill can be handled in two ways.

    A. Have each runner stride until he approaches the zone and then accelerate to full speed for the pass.

    B. Have each man run at full speed for the entire distance. This may or may not be a time trial.

7. Lane Drill (440 Relay)—Have the runners practice the passes using the different lanes on the track. This will prepare them to run in any lane during competition.

8. Circuit Drill (440 Relay)—Break up into groups of four. Have each runner pass and receive six times, then jog to the next passing zone. Repeat until all zones have been practiced.

9. Crowd Drill—Line up three or more passers and receivers. Upon a command by the coach, the passers should start together and complete their pass. The purpose of this drill is to get used to passing in crowded situations.

10. Catch-Up Drill—Have a "rabbit" runner take about a 10-yard running lead. The two relay runners will complete the pass and the receiver will sprint to catch the rabbit. The teaching point to emphasize here is that no matter how much distance must be made up, a good pass is still the first necessity.

11. Efficiency Drill—The coach times the pass from when the passer enters the zone until the receiver leaves the zone. The times can be used for comparison, evaluation, and improvement.

Since relays offer valuable benefits, it is important that coaches spend the time to perfect them. Not only do relays provide valuable points toward winning meets, but they are of great spectator interest and provide good team competition in a rather individualized sport. While speed and athletic ability are still important, a relay team can improve immensely by the combined efforts of coach and athletes in perfecting the techniques of relay running.

10 *Guidelines to Improve Running Posture*

One of the mistakes sometimes made in the coaching profession is that of limiting the athlete to one specific way of performing a skill or event. The skill of running, as basic as it may seem, is a victim of this abuse. Much of the literature on the correct way to run leads one to believe that all runners must run or sprint in identical fashion. This is not true. Individual differences among runners should be taken into consideration. Running form is general, while running posture is specific to the individual. Each person is said to have a standing, sitting, and walking posture. When applicable, this should include a running posture. Body type and structure determine much of how a person will look and move as well as other factors such as height, weight, natural strength, endurance, size of muscular bulk, and even personality.

Posture will differ not only according to body types, but in the different running events. While general similarities do not change, a sprinter during the 100 yard dash does not run with the same posture as if he were running a mile. Posture can change within the individual depending on the type of running he is performing. A runner actually possesses two postures. One is for sustained running and the other for sprinting. The form and general characteristics for these movements will also differ to some extent. While man is a land animal, the skill of running is not completely natural to him. Running form is best taught and posture developed in the elementary school years. Too often the basic fundamental skills are neglected in the growing child and specific sport skills are substituted and taught in their place. This can rob the youth of his opportunity to choose his athletic endeavor and is especially detrimental to the potential track and cross-country athlete. Habits are formed in the growing years and become increasingly hard to break as the athlete gets older. However, every attempt should be made to help a runner attain the best possible running posture regardless of his age or level of competition.

RUNNING POSTURE DEFINED

Though the running movement is complex, it does not have to be difficult for the athlete. While the coach should know all the aspects of running, it is best not to confuse the athlete with that which does not apply to him. Posture can be acquired through practice, but too much concentration or change is probably as harmful as none. In other words, do not make the runner feel that he is doing something wrong if some of his posture traits do not conform exactly to textbook standards. The overall action of the run must be considered first.

The following definitions may help to clarify some common terms used in discussing the running movement.

Mechanics of Running. The anatomical and kinesiological actions and coordination of the different parts of the body during the running movement.

Running Form. Characteristics or actions of the running movement which are general to the construction of the human body, but not specific to individual differences and body types.

Running Posture. A runner's use of mechanics and form that are specific to individual differences and body types.

Style. An acquired characteristic or trait of running posture.

IMPORTANCE OF POSTURE

The main objective of improving running posture is to improve performance. By developing the traits that best suit him, an athlete can run more efficiently. Posture need not be attractive or pleasing to the eye as long as it is efficient. If an athlete is running well and attempts to alter his posture have not improved his performance, by all means leave him alone. Do not force form on him. Once the athlete becomes confused or awkward in his running, he may alter his natural posture to the extent that his running is hampered. Success in running is not always characterized by perfect form.

Efficient running takes place when there is no unnecessary movement or wasted effort. In other words, energy should be expended only to produce the best running movement possible. By conserving energy, many of the other mechanics of running are made easier. There are successful runners who appear to be wasting energy by their actions, but are really compensating for the lack of another trait of form. The overall body action must be viewed in regard to one's posture. The whole must be analyzed before the part. In examining a runner's whole action, the following guidelines are suggested:

1. How successful is the runner at present?
2. Is he running naturally?
3. Does he appear to be wasting effort or using unnecessary movements?
4. What is his running background?
5. Have there been previous attempts at posture change?
6. Does he appear relaxed and satisfied with his present posture?

THE COACH'S ROLE IN IMPROVING POSTURE

A good rule for the running coach to follow concerning posture is to learn everything there is about it and impart very little of it. The role of the coach is to examine, analyze, and make suggestions for improvement. If a posture problem exists, work for a change; but runners should not be experimented upon or forced to do it the "right way." Many prominent running authorities will agree—offer help only to those who need help. Do not tamper with that which is successful. The dedicated athlete will be enthusiastic about any possibility of improving his performance, so there is no need to be overzealous or fanatical in the approach to posture and style. The art of coaching runners requires a sensitive approach that is creative and positive. Negativism should be avoided. Instead of "No! That isn't right." try using expressions such as "I think we can improve upon ——— by trying this." A positive psychological approach will usually gain better results than negative methods. The successful coach can usually distinguish what is important from what is unimportant. This is a skill that results from experience.

RELAXATION

To be able to run relaxed and still maintain maximum effort is one of the goals of all runners. The absence of relaxation is caused by tension and stress. Both of these conditions can cause a change in muscular contraction while running, as well as produce premature fatigue. Complete relaxation is defined as the absence of neuromuscular activity. While this is not possible during running, it is feasible to perform the running movement with as little tension as possible. In chapter 12, relaxation techniques and drills are described for use during running to aid the athlete in preventing the tightening up of the musculature and premature fatigue.

Much of the tension prior to competition or training is psychological. Learning to relax before running is a motor skill which should be practiced by those runners who find preliminary tension a handicap to their performance.

The following relaxation program can be used for tension release prior to competition or training.

1. Start with the usual warm-up. This should include jogging, light calisthenics, and flexibility exercises.
2. About twenty minutes prior to running, the athletes should do the following: (Length of time may vary with the individual.)
    A. Place a rolled towel or sweat shirt under the neck and lie flat on your back. The arms are extended to the side and the legs flat and apart.
    B. Respiration. Take a deep breath and exhale slowly letting the chest depress as far as it will go. Repeat slowly, three times or more, then resume normal breathing.
    C. Abdominals. Tighten or contract the abdominal muscles, hold for three seconds and release. Repeat twice.
    D. Lower Leg. Curl the toes downward and extend the feet flexing the calf muscles. Release and curl the toes upward flexing the foot and extending the calf muscles. Release and repeat twice.
    E. Upper Leg. With the feet slightly apart and the toes pointed, the legs are raised about six inches off the ground and kept straight. Held for five seconds, this should cause tension in the upper thighs. Release and repeat twice.
    F. Hips. With the feet slightly apart, draw the hips up to a flexed position, (hip flexor) creating tension at the bend of the hip. Release and repeat twice.

G. Lower Back. Raise the hips slightly and tighten the gluteal muscles. Release and repeat twice.

H. Upper Back, Shoulders. Shrug both shoulders up, back, and down. Return by shrugging up, forward, and down. Release and repeat the double movement twice.

I. Shoulders, Arms, Hands, Fingers. Using a tight fist, bend both arms at the elbow and flex lifting the upper arm off the ground and curling the arms towards the middle of the chest. Release and repeat twice.

J. Neck. Bend the head forward toward the chest and hold. Now bend the head backward and then turn from side to side quickly. Repeat twice.

K. Head, Face. Keep the mouth and teeth tightly together. Force a wide smile using as many parts of the face as possible. Release slowly. Repeat twice.

3. Lie completely still for about five minutes. This should produce relaxation prior to running.

Notes on Program

1. As each specific exercise tenses a certain part of the body, the other parts should be kept in a relaxed state.

2. Perform the exercises slowly and correctly. The exercises given should be comfortably done in five minutes plus the five minute still relaxation period.

3. After the first exercise for respiration, breathing should be kept slow and regular.

4. During this program, the mind should concentrate on producing relaxation.

5. In some cases, the entire program may not be needed. Some athletes may respond well to two or three exercises.

MECHANICS AND FORM FOR SUSTAINED RUNNING

Leg Action

The leg action is divided into two phases: Pulling and pushing. The pulling action takes place after the foot has made contact with the ground, supported the bodyweight, and caused a change in the center of body gravity. As the center of gravity changes and the other leg moves forward towards the next stride, the pulling begins as the leg leaves the ground and begins to lift preparing for its next stride. The pull continues through the recovery and the knee lift until the leg extends to make contact with the ground again. The pushing action begins with the extended leg and as contact is made. The leg then pushes off moving the center of body gravity forward. This pushing or driving action causes propulsion of the body and provides the power in running. The pushing action ends as that leg leaves the ground and becomes the trail leg. There is a brief period of inertia or suspension when neither leg is actually touching the ground. This period should be kept as brief as possible as power or drive can be lost.

Foot Placement

Ideally the foot should make first contact on the outside edge, recoil lightly off the heel and roll high up on the ball of the foot with the toes pulled upward after ground contact. This contact should be made with the lead foot at or slightly ahead of the center of the body's gravity. There may be slight variations to this movement as a result of individual postures. However, most research has shown that runners usually make contact first with the outside of the foot regardless of the pace involved, but that the pace of the race is the determining factor for foot placement.

Knee Lift

The knee lift should be a forward projection and is part of the pulling phase of the leg action. A general rule to follow for the amount of knee lift is that the knee be lifted only high enough to obtain the maximum stride length desired for the speed being run.

Trail Leg Lift

The trailing leg movement is one of the most natural in a runner's posture. Some authorities emphasize that the trial leg should never recoil above a parallel position with the knee. However the amount of body lean and the speed being run often distort this angle. The strength and flexibility of the runner also influence this movement. Unless the trial leg lift is causing a posture problem, it is probably best left alone providing it is a natural and relaxed movement.

Stride Length

The length of the runner's stride is related most to the speed being run and such physical traits as size, strength, and flexibility. The stride length should be a natural movement relative to the runner's posture and speed. However an increase in stride length without decreasing the rate of leg movement will increase running speed.

Body Alignment

For sustained running, the angle of body lean is nearly erect. A faster rate of speed or excessive wind resistance will tend to exaggerate the body lean, but it is safe to say that most successful runners maintain as near an erect posture as possible. The point for checking the body lean of a runner is just as the lead leg makes contact with the ground. The purpose of any forward body lean is to move the center of body gravity ahead of the pushing or driving action of the legs.

Arm Action

The swinging or rotary arm movement aids in the overall balance of the body during running. The overall arm action projects forward motion. The upper arm moves forward and backward in a straight motion with the elbows kept into the sides. The lower arm, held in a near-parallel position with the ground, reacts with the upper arm and shoulder movement but moves slightly across the body. This crossing motion should not extend past the vertical midline of the body. This will shift the position of the center of body gravity, thus causing imbalance. The arms should move in an alternate synchronization with the speed of the legs and generally should not be allowed to drop lower than hip level in erect posture. It has been stated that when the upper body and arm movements are correct for the individual's posture, the legs will function properly. The coordination and effectiveness of the arm action can benefit from the use of strength training.

Hand Position

The main characteristic of any hand position is that it be relaxed and free from strain or tension. During the arm action, the hands will tend to turn with the wrist movement. This should not be corrected as long as it is natural. A suggested technique for the hands is to keep them in a semi-closed or cupped position and place the thumb directly into the side of the middle section of the forefinger. This technique allows free movement of the hands and wrist, yet maintains control without causing tension.

Head Position

The position of the head should be in natural alignment with the amount of body lean. The head should rest loosely on the shoulders with the eyes focused straight ahead. The head can turn from side to side for purposes of direction and balance but should not be thrown either forward or back as this can change the entire running posture of the body.

MECHANICS AND FORM FOR SPRINTING

The basic definition of a sprint is a race that requires an all out effort at all times. Sprinting posture is very individual, and correct form is usually attributed to the fastest runners. The mechanics and form for sprinting differ only slightly from those of sustained running. To avoid repetition, the following material will present only the variations.

Leg Action

At the start of a sprint, the rear leg drives forward on the first stride as far as possible, with the foot landing at the center of body gravity. The length of the stride will depend upon the size and body type of the runner. The knees are carried through forward and fast in order to keep under the body's weight. Upon surface contact, the landing is on the balls of the feet with the first contact being made on the outside edge. The feet are pointed directly towards the line of run. The driving time off the toes is shortened by pulling the toes upward towards the knee immediately after contact occurs.

Once the sprinter has attained maximum speed or acceleration, the knee is lifted only high enough to obtain the maximum stride length. The foreleg must also be extended for this purpose. The sprinter should always run high on his toes and project himself forward instead of up.

The finish of a sprint requires no change in the leg action, in fact emphasis should be placed at this time on maintaining one's posture and not decelerating or pulling up too soon.

Body Alignment

Faster speeds require more body lean, mainly due to acceleration and increased wind resistance. However, the lean still should not be exaggerated. At the finish of a sprint if a lunge or shrug is used, the sprinter should be careful not to suddenly straighten up before making such a movement as this will have a definite slowing effect upon his speed. Many sprinters appear to stand straight or even lean slightly backward at the finish. This is due to deceleration. It is not possible to continually accelerate during an entire run at top speed. Therefore deceleration will occur in all sprinters after reaching top speed and maintaining it briefly, thus affecting the angle of body lean.

Arm Action

Upon starting, the opposite arm to the lead leg should be thrust forward quickly to accelerate the upper body movement and direction. As in sustained running, the arm action governs the quality of the leg drive during the pushing action. The position of the arms and hands is basically the same.

Head Position

The head is held in the natural position. The eyes are focused straight ahead. The head and back should form a nearly straight line. During the sprint start, the head should not be lifted. This will cause the runner to straighten up too quickly and lose power. Irregular head movements during sprinting can upset the body alignment and the center of body gravity. The face, jaws, and neck should be as relaxed as possible.

COMMON POSTURE-RELATED FAULTS (ALPHABETICAL ORDER)

Arms Crossing Vertical Plane of Body. This results in a constant shifting of the center of body gravity and causes the athlete to run unbalanced. It also hampers the forward projection of the running action.

Arms and Hands Held Too Low. The runner who dangles or does not control the position of the arms and hands will not be able to get the most benefit from the arm action. It may also cause posture problems in the synchronization of the leg action.

Excessive Body Lean. This will cause a shift in the center of body gravity and can shorten stride length.

Excessive Head Lift. This is most noticeable during the finish of a run. Lifting the head backwards will cause a loss of speed and a shorter stride length.

Excessive Head Tilt. Usually caused by fatigue, letting the head fall forward can shift the center of body gravity and possibly cause the athlete to lose balance and fall.

Excessive Knee Lift. This causes a slower rate of leg movement and wastes effort.

Excessive or Unnatural Arm Action. This can cause synchronization problems with the leg action, wastes effort, and may shift the center of body gravity.

Foot Pounding. A lack of strength may cause this unnecessarily hard contact with the running surface. It can result in a loss of speed and stride length as well as possible injury to the foot and lower leg.

Hands Tightly Clenched. This creates tension in the upper body, causes premature fatigue, and a loss of relaxation.

Overstriding. This is characterized by a slow down in the rate of leg movement and a loss of speed. The runner spends too much time without surface contact. Overstriding is caused primarily by overextension and reaching with the legs, which takes away from the pushing or driving action.

Running Straight Up. This will cause a shorter stride length as well as a loss of speed. It is characterized by a running movement that bounces up and down rather than projecting forward.

Running with the Feet Turned Outward. In most people this is a completely unnatural movement. The runner pushes off on the inside of the foot and big toe instead of all the toes and the ball of the foot. Injury to the foot and lower leg may result.

Tense Arm Action. This will inhibit the synchronization of the leg action and cause a loss of relaxation while running.

Understriding. A shortened stride length will cause a loss of speed, create tension, and inhibit the running movement. Understriding is characterized by running up and down instead of forward and projects a strained image during running.

Running posture is specific to the body type and needs of the individual while mechanics and form are general to all. Efficient posture is not identical for all. It is primarily a natural action, but can be improved through knowledge and practice. The successful coach will use good judgement as to those characteristics of a runner that need improvement and those which should be left unchanged. He must be careful not to fit everyone into the same mold, even if it has proven successful for others. By improving posture, we improve performance. It is necessary to understand the mechanics and form of running for use in observing and improving running posture.

11 How to Organize and Coach Strength Training for Runners

WHY STRENGTH TRAINING FOR RUNNERS?

Research into the area of strength training has shown without a doubt that it is beneficial in the development of strength, power, flexibility, speed, and muscular endurance. The outdated idea that strength training adds unwanted weight, decreases speed, and is harmful to any sport where running speed, agility, and reaction time are important is completely unwarranted.

As coaches, we are always looking for methods to use which will improve upon the natural ability of the athlete. Strength training is one such method. The theory for runners is that by building or adding strength, speed and endurance will be increased, which in turn will improve performances on the course or track. Strength, once acquired, can be maintained with minimal work. The strength program will vary with the running seasons. The more strenuous work will be done in the off-season and preseason training, while the in-season program will provide for strength maintenance. The musculature of the upper body plays an important part in running. While the legs are used most, these other areas should not be overlooked.

A strength program for runners should provide the following:

1. A workout that is pertinent to the event(s).
2. A workout that will not interfere with the regular practice.
3. A workout that will benefit strength development but not cause undue fatigue in the athlete.
4. A workout that is based on sensible strength training principles.

It should be emphasized that the strength workout is not a substitute for practice or any other training phase. It is to be considered as a part of the total training to improve running performance.

Strength is developed progressively. To increase strength, the resistance must be increased. The athlete must exert full effort into his program. Strength training based upon sound physiological and kinesthetic principles is the only way strength will be successfully developed and maintained. Any program advocating instant strength or radical methods of training should not be considered for use in athletics.

The results of strength training probably will not enable a five minute miler to break four minutes, but it should help the runner in reaching his maximum potential. Some of the benefits that *can* result from strength training are:

1. Increase in muscular strength.
2. Increase in muscular endurance.
3. Increase in speed of movement.
4. Increase in running speed.
5. Increase in power.
6. Increase in flexibility.
7. Increase in agility.
8. Increase in reaction time.
9. Increase in the quality of a muscle.

Strength is basic to athletic skill. Many other athletic factors can be compensated for by the possession of strength. All muscular performance becomes easier with strength.

PRINCIPLES OF STRENGTH TRAINING

Types of Strength

1. Dynamic strength pertains to the maximum load that can be moved once.
2. Explosive strength is the ability to exert maximum effort into one explosive act.
3. Enduring strength involves repetition of an act with high or low intensity work.

Strength is the ability of a muscle to produce tension in a moving or non-moving manner. Muscular contraction provides the basis for this act. The potential of a muscle to produce tension is based on three factors:

1. The size and quality of the muscle.
2. The number and rate of impulses sent by the nervous system.

3. Psychological inhibitory factors that would restrict the ability of a muscle to produce maximum tension.

Running is most concerned with enduring and explosive strength; however, dynamic strength, which is gained by progressive resistance in strength training, will be developed also. The three types of strength are closely interrelated in training and their effects on running performance. A runner must be strong in initial movement such as the sprint start, in sustained efforts as in distance running, and in the ability to exert maximum effort when needed, even while facing fatigue.

Strength is a factor in many of the techniques used for increasing running speed. When a muscle is working to its fullest capacity, the trained or stronger muscle works with less effort and more efficiency than an untrained muscle. The recuperation of a trained muscle is faster, therefore muscular fatigue will not affect its performance as it does the untrained muscle.

Power

Power equals force times velocity. It is the application of strength and speed during a muscular movement. Power is most closely related to dynamic and explosive strength. The added dimension is quickness of movement. In any muscular movement, the force of gravity and/or inertia must be overcome. Strength, power, and speed are closely related. Power is more important to the sprint events, as the force they encounter at faster rates of speed and quicker starts is heavier than that of the middle-distance and distance events. The longer the event, the more important physical endurance becomes. While all strength training helps develop power, training with a higher number of sets, few repetitions, and heavy resistance is best. Physical testing of Olympic athletes showed that the competitive weight lifter was the fastest man by speed of movement. Also shown was that weight trained athletes were faster than those who did not weight train. This information serves to emphasize the importance of strength and power to the track athlete. In any running competition, if all other factors are equal, the stronger athlete will have the advantage.

Types of Strength Programs

Strength programs for athletics are generally classified into four categories. Since a program should be designed to fit the needs of a specific event or sport, it is not possible to utilize the same workouts throughout the year or to use the same for everyone. Certainly, a hurdler has different needs than a distance runner. The answer is to use separate strength training programs for different events and different phases of the season. The four categories are:

1. The Basic Program. A general workout for overall body strength. It's purposes are to condition the body for more strenuous training to follow and to provide a starting program for the beginning trainee. The basic program is characterized by a variety of exercises and light to moderate resistance. It is best utilized prior to a specific strength program, or after a training layoff.

2. The Specific Program. This program should be directed to specific training for the task to be performed. As it may not possess the variety of a basic program, it should not be considered a complete power program. After the basic program has conditioned the athlete, the specific program should be employed until about two weeks before the competitive season begins.

3. The Maintenance Program. The purpose of a strength maintenance program is to maintain the strength and power that an athlete has built up during his prior training. A maintenance or in-season program will also serve as a preventive for certain types of injuries. It should be used two or three times weekly during the competitive season, but should not cause prolonged fatigue at any time.

4. The Rest Period. At some time during the training, preferably as the competitive season ends, the strength training should be discontinued temporarily to allow the body to rest before taking on new goals and resuming training. This should not be for a longer period of time than thirty days. During this rest, the athlete should remain mildly active.

Strength Terminology (Alphabetical Order)

The following terms are related to strength training and pertain to the programs given in this chapter.

1. *Breathing*—There is much controversy about how to breathe during strength training. A general rule to follow is to inhale on the pulling phase and exhale on the pushing phase. The athlete should not hold

his breath during any phase of strength training. Excessive deep breathing and breath holding can cause dizziness, nausea, or fainting if hyperventilation occurs.

2. *Circuit Training*—A training system in which a combination of exercises are performed consecutively for a designated number of repetitions or length of time. The circuit may be repeated as desired or be designed to be a complete workout.

3. *Countdown Training*—A training system in which the repetitions of each exercise are progressively decreased for each set or circuit throughout the workout. The workload or resistance is increased as the repetitions decrease or can remain constant.

4. *Isometric*—Muscular contraction with force exerted against an immovable object.

5. *Isotonic*—Muscular contraction with force exerted against a movable object.

6. *Maximum Effort Routine*—A workout routine in which each exercise is performed for one set to exhaustion. There should be little rest between exercises.

7. *Maximum Load Repetition (MLR)*—The heaviest amount of resistance that can be lifted for a specific exercise one time.

8. *Muscular Endurance Training*—A training method which involves few sets, high repetitions, and a fast speed of movement for an endurance effect on the muscles.

9. *Overload Principle*—The muscles must be forced to work beyond that point at which the task can be easily performed.

10. *Power Training*—A training method to improve strength and power. It is characterized by the use of heavy work loads, high sets, and low repetition. Due to the heavy resistance, the speed of movement for power training should be moderate and constant.

11. *Progressive Repetition*—A training system in which each consecutive set or circuit has a higher number of repetitions than the previous one. The workload or resistance does not change.

12. *Progressive Resistance Principle*—The resistance or workloads must be increased periodically based on the increased strength of the muscle.

13. *Repetition*—Each complete movement of the designated exercise within a set.

14. *Resistance/Workload*—The amount of weight that the athlete is lifting for each specific exercise.

15. *Rest Interval*—The amount of time taken between exercises, circuits, or sets to recuperate.

16. *Set*—A designated number of repetitions performed consecutively.

17. *Set System*—A training system in which each exercise is performed

in consecutive sets to the completion of the exercise. The number of repetitions within the sets remains the same, while the resistance can vary.

18. *Speed of Movement*—Pertains to the rate of speed at which each repetition of an exercise is performed.

19. *Starting Weight*—The workload or resistance that an athlete uses in beginning an exercise. While percentages and suggested work loads are given, experimentation and trial and error are sometimes best in establishing starting weight.

ORGANIZATION OF THE STRENGTH PROGRAM

Facilities and Equipment

Most strength programs are conducted in the gymnasium, all purpose room, special exercise room, or team room. A strength training facility should be well lighted, well ventilated, and have a solid surface. The size and structure of the area will dictate the placement of equipment. In some warm climates, strength training has been used out of doors. However, the ideal facility would provide for a permanent setup of the equipment to save time and make supervision less difficult.

The programs in this chapter can be used with barbells or many types of isotonic strength machines. If both are available, the coach or athlete may have a preference as to which to use. The size of the facility and the amount of equipment available will be a determining factor as to how many athletes can train at one time.

Instruction and Supervision

The exercises should be taught to the athletes by a qualified instructor. The knowledge of the correct form and movement for each exercise is important. Diagrams or charts illustrating the exercises should be posted. Individual progress records for each athlete should be kept in the workout facility. The athlete should record his work loads, sets, and repetition for each workout. This will maintain consistency and progression within the program.

Group instruction should be given for all participating athletes to learn the exercises. Individual help will follow when needed. The instructor should make sure that the exercises are being performed correctly. Each exercise should be taught in the following manner:

1. Give a brief description of the exercise and what muscles of the body it develops.
2. Demonstrate the correct grip and starting position.
3. Demonstrate the exercise twice at a slow speed.
4. Emphasize any teaching points, breathing, etc.
5. Demonstrate about five repetitions at normal speed.
6. Explain and demonstrate any spotting or safety techniques.
7. Ask for questions—give any comments.

At this point or after the teaching of several exercises, the athletes should practice correct form with a minimum of resistance under the supervision of the instructor. Once the exercises are learned and the starting weights determined, supervision is minimal as long as safety procedures are observed. In some team situations the trainer is responsible for the administration of the program.

Exercises

The exercises contained in the programs in this chapter are listed in Table 11-1. These exercises can be used with barbells or strength machines. However, the exercises are named by their use with the barbells. If strength machines are used, some of the exercises will need to be adapted to fit the resources of the specific type of machine in use.

Time for Workouts

This will vary according to the school, the season, and the type of program being used. If possible, some consistency in the workout time should be maintained. At the secondary school level, most programs are administered by the coach during or after school at the school facility. In the case of large groups, it is better to split the athletes into alternate day routines by running ability or events.

Length of Workouts

Since time is always an important factor in planning practice, the length of time spent on strength training should be sufficient, yet not excessive. Each program contained in this chapter has a time limit which will reasonably and comfortably fit its performance.

TABLE 11-1
LIST OF EXERCISES FOR THE STRENGTH TRAINING PROGRAMS

1. Arm Curl
2. Bench Press
3. Bent Arm Pullover (With Barbell, Dumbbell, or Plate)
4. Bentover Rowing
5. Dip
6. Dumbbell or Plate Swing (Warm-up) (Illustration 11-1)
7. Front Squat (Illustration 11-2)
8. Head Strap
9. Hip Flexor (Illustration 11-3)
10. Lateral Overhead and Forward Raise (With Dumbbells) (Illustration 11-4)
11. Parallel Squat
12. Power Clean (Illustration 11-5)
13. Power Clean and Power Press (Illustration 11-6)
14. Power Clean and Standing Press
15. Power Press (Illustration 11-7)
16. Pullover and Press (Illustration 11-8)
17. Pull-up
18. Quarter Squat
19. Rise on toes
20. Seated Calf Raise (Illustration 11-9)
21. Seated Press
22. Shoulder Shrug
23. Sit-up
24. Standing Press
25. Standing Press Behind Neck
26. Straight Arm Pullover
27. Upright Rowing
28. Wrist Roller

11-1

DUMBBELL OR PLATE SWING

11-2

FRONT SQUAT

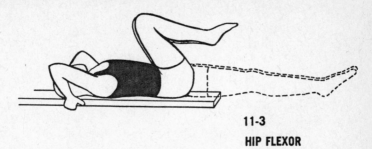

11-3
HIP FLEXOR

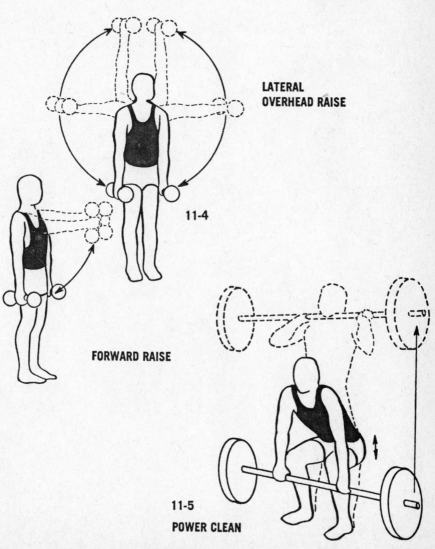

LATERAL
OVERHEAD RAISE

11-4

FORWARD RAISE

11-5
POWER CLEAN

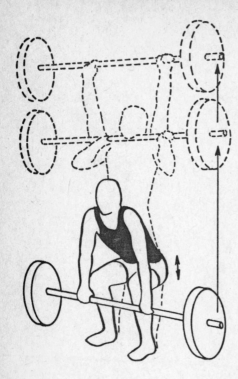

11-6

**POWER CLEAN AND
POWER PRESS
(COMBINATION EXERCISE)**

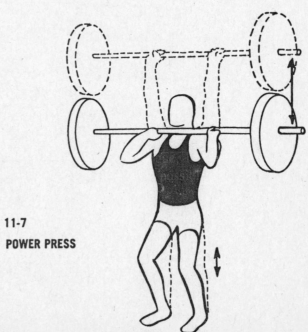

11-7

POWER PRESS

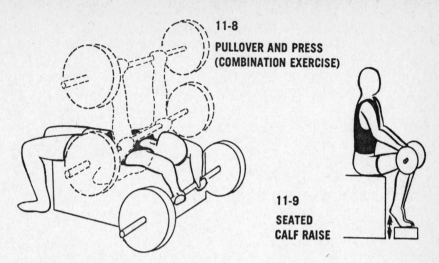

11-8
PULLOVER AND PRESS
(COMBINATION EXERCISE)

11-9
SEATED
CALF RAISE

Spotting and Safety

Athletes should not work alone on weight training equipment. It is best to have a partner. Some strength machines require no spotting, but for the sake of morale and motivation, it is still better not to train alone. Spotting serves two purposes. The first is to protect from injury while lifting and the second is to help in correct performance of the exercises. Spotting techniques for the barbells should be taught during the group instruction.

The following rules should be observed for safety in any strength training facility:

1. No horseplay of any kind.
2. Check equipment to make sure it is secure before using.
3. Replace or reset all equipment when finished.
4. Use spotters when necessary.
5. Athletes only! No spectators please.
6. Work out! Don't just talk about it.

Motivation

The main factor in motivating runners toward strength training is to impress upon them that it can improve their performance. Once a program has been established, the runners themselves will usually promote it. After the use of strength programs for some time, our runners were asked for their candid comments and feelings on its use. The following statements summarize their opinions:

1. Increased strength of the upper body makes running less tiring.
2. When fatigue does set in, the strength factor becomes important to give the maximum effort required.
3. Increased strength enables a fatigued runner to maintain running posture, utilize strength in running, and to finish stronger.
4. It is a simpler method, more compatible with running than isometrics or calisthenics.
5. It provides a complete variation from the normal training program.
6. It enhances appearance and improves self confidence, which are important psychological factors.

BASIC STRENGTH TRAINING FOR RUNNERS (OVERALL BODY STRENGTH)

Notes on the Basic Program

1. The workout should be performed three times weekly on alternate days.
2. The length of time for the workout should not exceed forty minutes.
3. The exercises should be performed in the given order. The entire circuit is to be completed once. Progressive repetition is used.
4. The rest interval between exercises should not exceed one minute.
5. Correct form should be used on all exercises . . . Do not perform CHEATS.
6. The basic strength program is designed to accompany a running program.

POWER TRAINING FOR SPEED IMPROVEMENT

Notes on the Power Training for Speed Improvement

1. The power routine should be performed two to three times weekly on alternate days.
2. The length of time for the workout should not exceed sixty minutes.
3. Weight loads may be increased anytime, but should be done sensibly and only when needed.
4. Correct form and technique should be emphasized at all times.
5. A lifting belt is recommended. Spotting is essential.
6. Strength will be based on how much the athlete can lift for one repetition (MLR).
7. Power training should not be used during the competitive season or with a highly intensified running program. It is best utilized during

BASIC STRENGTH TRAINING PROGRAM

EXERCISE	WEEKLY REPETITIONS			ADD EACH WEEK	ESTIMATED STARTING WEIGHT
	1st DAY	2nd DAY	3rd DAY		
1. Warm-up-Dumbbell or Plate Swing	10	10	10	0	10 lbs.
2. Bench Press-Regular Grip	10	11	12	5#	50% of bodyweight
3. Parallel Squat-Heels Lifted	10	11	12	5#	50% of BW
4. Bent Arm Pullover	10	11	12	2½#	20% of BW
5. Upright Rowing	8	9	10	2½#	33⅓% of BW
6. Bentover Rowing	8	9	10	5#	40% of BW
7. Seated Press	8	9	10	2½#	40% of BW
8. Arm Curls	8	9	10	2½#	33⅓% of BW
9. Sit-ups	25	25	25	3 repetitions	bodyweight
10. Bench Press-Wide Grip	8	9	10	5#	50% of BW
11. Parallel Squat-Flat Footed	10	11	12	5#	50% of BW
12. Rise on Toes	10	12	14	5#	50% of BW
13. Straight Arm Pullover	10	11	12	2½#	15% of BW
14. Upright Rowing	8	9	10	2½#	33⅓% of BW
15. Shoulder Shrug	10	12	14	2½#	40% of BW
16. Standing Press	8	9	10	2½#	40% of BW
17. Arm Curl	8	9	10	2½#	33⅓% of BW
18. Bench Press-Narrow Grip	8	9	10	5#	50% of BW
19. Quarter Squat	10	11	12	10#	75% of BW
20. Pull-ups	6	6	6	1 repetition	bodyweight
21. Dips	8	8	8	2 repetitions	bodyweight
22. Wrist Roller	Up and down twice			1¼#	10 lbs.
23. Sit-ups	25	25	25	3 repetitions	bodyweight

the off-season and early season, before the training becomes intense. A good example would be a sprinter power training in the fall.

8. The order in which the exercises are given is recommended, but can vary if necessary.

9. The number of sets given for each exercise is recommended as a minimum, yet sufficient in quantity for its purpose. Depending on the individual, an increase of sets may be warranted. However, in power training, the athlete must be careful not to overtrain. Tiredness, stiffness, and failure to recuperate fully are common signs of overtraining.

10. The purpose of the power routine is to work with the heaviest weight loads that the athlete can handle for the designated number of repetitions. Therefore, the weight loads should be increased as the number of repetitions is decreased for each exercise.

11. Once every six workouts, the athlete should test his MLR (maximum load repetition) for the bench press, parallel squat, power clean, and power press. This workout should include about five sets per exercise. No set should consist of more than three reps working down to single reps and the MLR. Weight loads should be planned for each set. It is recommended that the athlete not do all of them during the same workout. (Example: Do the bench press and parallel squat during one workout and the power clean and power press during the next workout.)

POWER TRAINING PROGRAM

EXERCISE	SETS	REPETITIONS
1. Warm-up-Dumbbell or Plate Swing	1	15
2. Bench Press	4	*10-5-5-5
3. Parallel Squat	4	*10-5-5-5
4. Seated Calf Raise	3	10-10-10
5. Bent Arm Pullover	2	10-10
6. Power Clean	3	5-5-5
7. Power Press	3	5-5-5
8. Arm Curl	3	7-7-7
9. Hip Flexor	1	25+
10. Sit-up	1	25+

*Light resistance set to insure complete warm up prior to the heavy resistance sets.

SPECIFIC STRENGTH TRAINING FOR RUNNERS

Notes on the Specific Program

1. The workout should be performed two to three times weekly on alternate days. It is designed to accompany the running program, but not during the competitive season. The number of times used weekly will depend upon the condition of the athlete and the intensity of his training.
2. The length of the workout should not exceed forty-five minutes.
3. The program is constructed by the set system with the principles of overload and progressive resistance. Resistance should be added as needed, but not more than once weekly. Weight loads should have been determined from the basic program.
4. Rest intervals between exercises should be kept to a minimum, not to exceed ninety seconds.
5. Correct form should be used on all exercises . . . Do not perform CHEATS.
6. The speed of movement for all exercises should be as fast as possible without sacrificing form. Fast movements build fast muscles.
7. WORKLOADS

    Light (L) High repetition (12 to 15) low resistance . . . should temporarily fatigue muscles causing a pumping effect . . . used for muscular endurance, recuperation should be rapid.

    Moderate (M) Moderate resistance . . . normal weight load from basic program . . . the last three repetitions of a set (8-10) should present a challenge.

    Heavy (H) Low repetition, high resistance . . . maximum repetition is six . . . each repetition should present a challenge, but not a maximum lift . . . should not cause fatigue or soreness.

SPECIFIC STRENGTH TRAINING
SPRINTERS' AND HURDLERS' PROGRAM

EXERCISE	SETS	REPETITIONS	RESISTANCE
1. Warm-up-Dumbbell or Plate Swing	1	15	10-25 lbs.
2. Bench Press	3	10-5-15	M-H-L
3. Parallel Squat	2	5-5	H-H
4. Front Squat	1	10	M
5. Bentover Rowing	2	10-10	M-M

EXERCISE	SETS	REPETITIONS	RESISTANCE
6. Seated Calf Raise	2	10-5	M-H
7. Bent Arm Pullover	2	10-10	M-M
8. Power Clean and Power Press	3	7-5-7	M-H-M
9. Upright Rowing	2	10-10	M-M
10. Lateral, Forward, Overhead Raise	1	21 (7 for each position)	L
11. Arm Curl	3	10-5-10	M-H-M
12. Hip Flexor	1	25+	Bodyweight
13. Sit-ups	1	25+	Bodyweight

SPECIFIC STRENGTH TRAINING
MIDDLE-DISTANCE RUNNERS' PROGRAM

EXERCISE	SETS	REPETITIONS	RESISTANCE
1. Warm-up-Dumbbell or Plate Swing	1	15	10-25 lbs.
2. Bench Press	3	10-5-10	M-H-M
3. Parallel Squat	2	10-5	M-H
4. Front Squat	1	10	M
5. Bentover Rowing	2	10-10	M-M
6. Seated Calf Raise	2	10-10	M-M
7. Bent Arm Pullover	2	10-10	M-M
8. Power Clean and Standing Press	2	7-7	M-M
9. Upright Rowing	2	10-10	M-M
10. Lateral, Forward, Overhead Raise	1	21 (7 for each position)	L
11. Arm Curl	3	10-5-10	M-H-M
12. Hip Flexor	1	25+	Bodyweight
13. Sit-ups	1	25+	Bodyweight

SPECIFIC STRENGTH TRAINING
CROSS-COUNTRY AND DISTANCE RUNNERS' PROGRAM

EXERCISE	SETS	REPETITIONS	RESISTANCE
1. Warm-up-Dumbbell or Plate Swing	1	15	10-25 lbs.
2. Bench Press	3	10-10-15	M-M-L
3. Parallel Squat	2	10-15	M-L
4. Bentover Rowing	2	10-15	M-L
5. Seated Calf Raise	2	10-10	M-M
6. Bent Arm Pullover	2	10-10	M-M
7. Power Clean and Standing Press	2	7-7	M-M

EXERCISE	SETS	REPETITIONS	RESISTANCE
8. Upright Rowing	2	10-15	M-L
9. Lateral, Forward, Overhead Raise	1	21 (7 for each position)	L
10. Arm Curl	3	10-10-15	M-M-L
11. Hip Flexor	1	25+	Bodyweight
12. Sit-ups	1	25+	Bodyweight

IN-SEASON STRENGTH MAINTENANCE

Notes on the Maintenance Program

1. The workout should be performed two to three times weekly on alternate days. Do not work out 48 hours prior to competition.
2. The length of time for the workout should not exceed thirty minutes.
3. This strength maintenance program is designed for use during the competitive season.
4. Correct form should be used on all exercises . . . Do not perform CHEATS.
5. Add resistance as needed, not more than once weekly.
6. No leg work unless remedial exercise prescribed by trainer or doctor.
7. WORKLOADS

   Light (L) High repetition (12 to 15) low resistance . . . should temporarily fatigue muscles, causing a pumping effect . . . used for muscular endurance, recuperation should be rapid. The speed of each movement is fast.

   Moderate (M) Moderate resistance . . . normal weight load . . . the last three repetitions of a set (8-10) should present a challenge. The speed of movement should be as fast as possible.

   Heavy (H) Low repetition, high resistance . . . maximum repetition is six . . . each repetition should present a challenge, but not a maximum lift . . . should not cause fatigue or soreness.
8. The entire circuit is to be completed once. The advantages of circuit training for strength maintenance are:
   A. The programs can be performed more rapidly with shorter rest intervals between exercises.
   B. The circuit is expedient. It enables a larger number of athletes to train at the same time on the same equipment.
   C. It discourages excessive work on any one exercise.
   D. Circuit training applies the principle of progressive resistance.
   E. Research shows that circuit training is more beneficial toward strength maintenance for a specialized athletic activity.

TABLE 11-2
INTEGRATION OF STRENGTH TRAINING

	SEPTEMBER	OCTOBER	NOVEMBER	DECEMBER	JANUARY	FEBRUARY
Sprinters (100-220-440) and Hurdlers (Highs, Lows, Intermediate)	BASIC POWER	POWER	POWER	POWER SPECIFIC	SPECIFIC	SPECIFIC MAIN-TENANCE
Runners of All Other Distances NOT Participating in Cross-country	BASIC	POWER OR SPECIFIC	POWER OR SPECIFIC	SPECIFIC	SPECIFIC	MAIN-TENANCE
Runners of All Other Distances Participating in Cross-country	MAIN-TENANCE	MAIN-TENANCE	MAIN-TENANCE	BASIC	SPECIFIC	SPECIFIC MAIN-TENANCE

	MARCH	APRIL	MAY	JUNE	JULY	AUGUST
Sprinters (100-220-440) and Hurdlers (Highs, Lows, Intermediate)	MAIN-TENANCE	MAIN-TENANCE	MAIN-TENANCE	MAIN-TENANCE	REST	BASIC
Runners of All Other Distances NOT Participating in Cross-country	MAIN-TENANCE	MAIN-TENANCE	MAIN-TENANCE	MAIN-TENANCE	REST	BASIC
Runners of All Other Distances Participating in Cross-country	MAIN-TENANCE	MAIN-TENANCE	MAIN-TENANCE	REST	BASIC	SPECIFIC

IN-SEASON STRENGTH MAINTENANCE
SPRINTERS' AND HURDLERS' PROGRAM

EXERCISE	REPETITIONS	RESISTANCE
1. Bench Press	10	M
2. Bentover Rowing	10	M
3. Upright Rowing	10	M
4. Power Clean and Power Press	8	M
5. Arm Curl	10	M
6. Hip Flexor	25+	Bodyweight
7. Bench Press	5	H
8. Bent Arm Pullover	10	M
9. Shoulder Shrug	10	M
10. Bentover Rowing	12	L
11. Standing Press Behind Neck	12	L
12. Arm Curl	12	L
13. Pullover and Press	12	L
14. Sit-ups	25+	Bodyweight

IN-SEASON STRENGTH MAINTENANCE
CROSS-COUNTRY, MIDDLE-DISTANCE,
AND DISTANCE RUNNERS' PROGRAM

EXERCISE	REPETITIONS	RESISTANCE
1. Bench Press	10	M
2. Bentover Rowing	10	M
3. Upright Rowing	10	M
4. Seated Press	10	M
5. Arm Curl	10	M
6. Hip Flexor	25+	Bodyweight
7. Bench Press	15	L
8. Straight Arm Pullover	12	L
9. Bentover Rowing	12	L
10. Shoulder Shrug	10	M
11. Standing Press Behind Neck	12	L
12. Arm Curl	12	L
13. Pullover and Press	12	L
14. Sit-ups	25+	Bodyweight

INTEGRATION OF STRENGTH PROGRAMS

Table 11-2 illustrates the suggested use and integration of strength training into the running year for a program which can include cross-country, an indoor and an outdoor season. Since each coach knows his own program, athletes, and schedule best, he is the one who should determine the length of time for each phase of the strength training and integrate it to successfully fit the needs of his runners.

There is no substitute for a solid running program and a runner who trains hard. However, strength training can be a valuable supplement to any program. The athletic world has accepted the fact that strength training is important as supplementary training and is beneficial in the development of the running athlete. The runner can develop and use strength to improve his performance without any negative side effects by the use of a properly planned program.

12 *Programs to Improve Running Speed*

CAN SPEED BE IMPROVED?

Can speed be improved? The answer is emphatically yes. It has been established through research that speed can be improved. This is accomplished through various training methods. Certain physical factors such as heredity, natural strength, flexibility, and body measurements do offer some limitations for the athlete, but it is possible to say that the speed of any athlete can be increased.

Too much emphasis is often placed on the inherent physical characteristics of an individual and not enough time is spent in developing the qualities that will improve speed. The athlete possessed with natural speed is often the victim of this neglect and is deprived of the opportunity to improve his speed. Many coaches are unwilling to experiment or tamper with the speed of an already fast runner. It is relatively difficult to destroy one's natural speed by the use of proven training programs. The concept of the delicate sprinter should be discarded. However, any type of crash or "instant success" speed program should be avoided. These are the occasional causes for an athlete's setback in running speed. Whether it be strength training, flexibility exercises, or various running techniques, the programs used for speed improvement should be based upon sound, fundamental physiological and kinesiological principles. The improvement of speed is a gradual process. Overnight gains cannot be expected. Too often if immediate goals are not obtained, speed programs are discarded. It is not realistic to expect an 11 second—100 yard dash time to drop to 9.8. It would be more realistic to take the 9.8 runner and work him towards a 9.6.

Speed programs are not just designed for sprinters. Every runner needs speed. Middle and long-distance runners can benefit from speed programs also. For them speed is not just a finishing kick, but relates more to their entire race. They need a "fast or quick" leg just as sprinters do. Improvement of speed will not only increase their performance, but will tend to cause less strain in running.

Speed improvement is not restricted to the track athlete. These same programs can be of benefit to any athlete in the running sports such as football, basketball, soccer, baseball, and lacrosse.

ANALYSIS OF SPEED

The most important point in analyzing speed is that it is specific to the task. In other words, to use speed effectively, speed must be practiced. Regardless of what event the athlete is training for, speed or sprint work should be used to obtain the best results. There is no running event in track or cross-country in which, all other factors being equal, the faster athlete does not have the advantage.

Table 12-1 shows the variety of factors that are involved with speed. The control and improvement of these factors are most important in the speed process. Speed and its improvement rest upon the athlete's status concerning his physiological and psychological well-being as well as his training program and physical condition.

TABLE 12-1
FACTORS THAT ARE INVOLVED WITH THE IMPROVEMENT OF SPEED

PHYSIOLOGICAL	PSYCHOLOGICAL	TECHNICAL (Specific to Running)	ADDITIONAL
1. Strength	1. Stress	1. Stride Length	1. Diet
2. Power	2. Motivation	2. Rate of Leg Movement	2. Rest
3. Flexibility	3. Fatigue	3. Running Posture	3. Health Status
4. Agility	4. Pain	4. Warm-up	4. Injury Status
5. Reaction Time	5. Fear	5. Training Programs	5. Ergogenic Aids
6. Physical Endurance	6. Boredom	6. Training Conditions	

AREAS FOR SPEED IMPROVEMENT

Stride Length

Speed can be improved by increasing the length of the running stride while maintaining the same rate of leg movement. A trained runner will usually have a longer stride by 7 to 8 inches over an untrained runner. Stride length can be an acquired skill. Success in speed has been attributed to having a long stride that carries the runner low to the ground. The common fault regarding stride length is overstriding. Overstriding does not produce a faster rate of speed. Stride length can definitely be affected by strength training, flexibility training and specific running techniques.

Rate of Leg Movement

The rate of leg movement is determined by the quickness with which the runner moves his legs. This depends on excellent running posture. Agility and balance in regard to body position and leg placement are most important for an increase in the rate of leg movement. Speed is best obtained when the runner projects himself forward and not up and down. The knees should only move high enough to obtain the maximum stride length. Any extra knee lift wastes strength, energy, and time. The foot should land at the center of the body's gravity with the lower leg extended. The leg should be in a pushing and not a pulling motion. An increase in the rate of leg movement while not shortening the stride length is best accomplished by strength and power training, relaxation techniques, posture analysis and specific running techniques.

Strength—Power

Strength training for the legs and upper body appears to have a pronounced effect on running speed. Research has shown a strong relationship between strength, power, and speed. Strength development by the use of progressive resistance has shown improvements in running speed. Strength shows its greatest influence upon speed during the acceleration phase of running.

Power equals force times velocity. In other words, it is the application of strength and speed during a muscular movement. Speed related power could be termed "explosive." This adds the dimension of quickness to the movement. Strength is essential to the development of stride length and power to the rate of leg movement. Flexibility and reaction time are also aided by strength work. Caution should be taken that strength training is not a substitute for other types of training. It should be a supplement to the program.

Programs involving strength and power training for speed are covered in chapter 11.

Flexibility

Flexibility has a unique importance in athletics. Extensive flexibility is a quality of speed. The main result of increased flexibility is a longer stride length. However, flexibility training offers other benefits to the improvement of speed. It will:

1. Limit energy expenditure.
2. Assist in injury prevention.
3. Improve coordination.
4. Permit a freer arm movement.
5. Limit internal muscular resistance (tightening up).
6. Enable the athlete to exert strength through a full range of movement.

The main areas of flexibility important to running speed are the shoulders, hips, lower back, hamstrings, quadriceps of the legs, knees, and ankles.

Reaction Time

Reaction time is the lapse of time between the stimulus and the first muscular movement of the athlete. It has more relationship to sprinters and the sprint start than to the other running events. A sprinter's reaction time is usually less than that of a middle or long-distance runner. Reaction time can be improved, enabling the runner to begin movement faster. Some methods of improving reaction time are:

1. Increasing body strength.
2. Using the actual stimulus to start movement.
   (Example—Use of the gun to practice starts)
3. Improving running posture and physical endurance.
4. Using various reaction drills with the stimulus being sight, sound, movement, or imitation.

Running Posture

While this subject has been covered in chapter 10, it is important to emphasize again that a runner's posture should be analyzed and steps taken to improve or correct any faults or weaknesses. Relaxation techniques are especially useful in speed improvement when posture is a problem.

Physical Endurance

If an athlete's lack of physical endurance prevents him from working towards his maximum speed, a program of aerobic training followed by Fartlek is recommended before taking on any specific programs. Regardless of how long or strenuous the speed programs may be, they must be performed with efficiency involving one's best effort to obtain maximum results. This cannot be accomplished if the athlete becomes fatigued too easily.

Psychological Factors

Many psychological factors can be controlled to some extent by the coach. The method is called Psych Training or Training of the Mind and is becoming more widespread. The main purpose of this training is to help the athlete to bypass or overcome any psychological barriers that may hamper his performance. This depends upon recognition of the problem by the coach. The following suggestions may help in eliminating some of the psychological barriers that may develop concerning speed.

1. Discuss the techniques of training and speed programs with the athlete(s).
2. Use positive motivational techniques. Negativism can be self-defeating.
3. Provide training experiences that offer variation and challenge.
4. Use coach-athlete involvement in planning goals.
5. Provide supervision without authoritarianism.
6. Observe patience in obtaining goals.
7. Prepare the athlete for pain, soreness, stiffness, and fatigue which may occur.
8. Allow for individual differences in planning programs.

PROGRAMS FOR IMPROVING SPEED

Pump and Stride

A track, athletic field, or level surface area of about 110 yards in length is needed for this program.

1. WARM UP your runners with jogging and flexibility exercises until they are sufficiently loosened up to run at full speed.
2. HIGH KNEE PUMPS—3 REPETITIONS x 50 YARDS. Begin at full speed, bringing the knees as high as possible, while gradually moving forward until 50 yards is reached. Stop and walk back.
    A. For 50 yards, there should be about 100 high knee pumps or an average of 20 per 10 yards. Have the athletes count the number of pumps as they run until the approximate rate is reached.
    B. The interval of time between each run should not exceed two minutes.
    C. This phase should not take more than 10-12 minutes.
    D. When 50 yards becomes easy, increase to 75 yards and then 100 yards, maintaining the same rate of movement.
    Be sure the legs come up as high and as fast as possible!
3. Take a walking rest of five minutes.
4. JUMPING STRIDES—2 REPETITIONS × 100 YARDS. Begin with a normal stride and increase stride length until the runner is actually jumping each stride (about 60 yards). Continue the jumping stride until the 100 yards is completed. Stop and walk back.
    A. The interval of time between each run should not exceed three minutes.
    B. This phase should not take more than eight minutes.
5. The total workout exclusive of the warm-up should not exceed 25 minutes.
6. The workout should be performed three times weekly.

The Pump and Stride program can serve as a supplement to the regular training program and can be utilized during any phase of training. The combination of the high knee pumps for increasing the rate of leg movement and the jumping stride for an increase of stride length will result in an improvement of running speed.

Downhill Running

The hill or incline should be about 60 yards in length with a graded slope of about three to five degrees. The surface should be firm and the terrain smooth.

1. WARM UP your runners with jogging and flexibility exercises until they are sufficiently loosened up to run at full speed.
2. Start them at the top of the slope and run DOWN:
    A. As fast as possible and still maintain balance.
    B. Lengthening the running stride as much as possible.
    C. Using the other mechanics of running.

    D. Rest two minutes at the completion of the downhill run.

    E. This type of running will allow the runner to increase stride length, rate of leg movement, and develop relaxation in running, which in turn will improve speed.

3. Start them at the bottom of the slope and run UP:

    A. As fast as possible.

    B. Lifting the knees with a forward thrust.

    C. Using the other mechanics of running.

    D. Uphill running of this type develops power in speed.

4. Rest 2 minutes and repeat.

5. Start with 3 repetitions of the downhill-uphill run. Add one repetition each week until a maximum of 6 is reached.

6. This workout should be performed 3 times weekly. At a maximum of 6 repetitions, it should take no more than 25 minutes.

The program of Downhill Running can serve as part of or a supplement to the regular training program. It is best used after the runner is in good condition since the mechanics of running are very much involved.

Uphill Running

The hill should be graded between 15 and 30 degrees and anywhere in length from 40 to 60 yards. It is best if the hill can be circuited, so the runner need not stop or change direction.

1. WARM UP your runners with jogging and flexibility exercises until they are sufficiently loosened up to run at full speed.

2. Start them at the bottom of the hill and run UP:

    A. As fast as possible, exerting maximum effort.

    B. Lifting the knees and pushing forward, not bouncing up and down.

    C. Using the other mechanics of running.

3. At the top of the slope, jog DOWN the side of the hill and around until the UP starting point is reached. Repeat until the desired number of repetitions is completed. AT NO TIME WALK! The recovery jog should take no more than 90 seconds.

4. START WITH 300 YARDS OF UPHILL RUNNING (Example: Length of hill is 60 yards x 5 repetitions = 300 yards) and increase up to a maximum of 1000 yards as the training demands.

5. This program should be followed by a period of striding on a flat running surface and flexibility exercises for the legs to gain the full benefits of the workouts.

6. The program should be used 3 times weekly depending on the training schedule and the intensity of the workouts.

Uphill running improves speed through an increase in the rate of leg movement, leg strength and power, and physical endurance. It can serve as a training supplement or part of the regular program especially during off season training.

Acceleration Running

A track or athletic field may be used. Mark off 40, 80, and 120 yards.

1. WARM UP your runners with jogging and flexibility exercises until they are sufficiently loosened up to run at full speed.
2. THE ACCELERATION RUN:
   A. Run the first 40 yards at a comfortable stride, constantly increasing the pace.
   B. At the 40 yard mark, continue to accelerate to 80 yards constantly building up speed, but not full speed.
   C. At the 80 yard mark, have the runners make an all out effort to attain their top sprinting speed and continue through the 120 yard mark.
   D. As quickly as they can, the runners should decelerate, turn around, jog to the finish line, then WALK BRISKLY without stopping back to the start.
   E. REPEAT immediately until the desired number of repetitions is completed.
3. Start out with a minimum of 4 repetitions and work to a maximum of 16.

Acceleration Running will increase speed by improving running posture and physical endurance. Properly used, it will add leg strength, increase stride length and the rate of leg movement. Acceleration runs can be incorporated into the regular training schedule. They are an excellent means of conditioning at the end of a practice session and can be used daily.

Target Time Sprinting

A track or level surface area should be used for this program.

1. WARM UP your runners with jogging and flexibility exercises until they are sufficiently loosened up to run at full speed.
2. The distances best used for this program are between 40 and 60 yards. This should depend upon the condition of the athletes and can increase progressively by 5 or 10 yards.
3. RUN 10 REPETITIONS of the desired distance:
   A. Each sprint is to be timed and recorded.

    B. The runner can start on his own or an outside stimulus. However, this should be consistent.

    C. A one to two minute recovery interval is taken between sprints.

    D. Run THROUGH the finish line, do not slow down.

    E. Give maximum effort on each run.

4. ANALYSIS:

    A. The runner's target time should be established from an average of 3 previous time trials taken prior to beginning the program.

    B. The target time should be strived for as an average of the 10 runs.

    C. The times are added and then divided by 10 to establish the workout's pace. This is then compared to the target time.

    D. Consistency and advancement to a new target time are desired.

    E. Divide target time by the workout pace to establish a percentage of efficiency. Example: (40 yards in) $5.0 \div 5.4 = .92$. Athlete is running at 92% efficiency.

While this program is short in duration, it is highly stressful if maximum effort is exerted. It is mainly a program for sprint athletes. It can be performed two times weekly depending upon the regular training schedule. It may also be used as a testing or measurement instrument to check progress. The program improves speed through reaction time, running posture, leg strength and power, sprint repetition for physical endurance and anaerobic conditioning.

Relaxation Techniques

"Fighting" to increase speed or the tightening of the muscles can actually cause premature and rapid fatigue, thus decreasing speed. Relaxation is not characterized by a change in the mechanics of running. Mastery of proper relaxation prevents speed loss, tightening up, and fatigue, especially in the final yards of a run or sprint.

1. The body characteristics of relaxation are:

    A. HEAD—Head is held erect and natural. Do not throw head backward. Keep the jaw slightly open and loose. Do not tense or tighten facial or neck muscles.

    B. ARMS—Use normal arm movement keeping the hands semi-closed and loose. Do not clench fists or exaggerate excessive arm movements. Let the arms hang loosely and create a natural movement.

    C. BODY—Concentrate on keeping the back straight and the correct angle of body lean for the speed being run.

    D. LEGS—Relaxation will come naturally to the legs if the above characteristics are followed. The emphasis here is on posture and muscular movement. Overstriding can cause a loss of relaxation in running.

E. MIND—The mind can cause many problems while running. The athlete must concentrate on the task and blot out all other stimuli. By doing this, full attention can be given to the mechanics of running. The mind should be focused ONLY on the task being performed.

2. METHODS OF RELAXATION:

A. MODIFIED ACCELERATION RUNNING—Begin at a slow pace and gradually build up to maximum speed. Hold this speed for about 15 yards, then decelerate. A distance of about 100 yards is usually sufficient. While progressing to top speed, concentrate on posture and relaxation. It should be easy to see how it is possible to accelerate without "fighting" to increase speed. Upon deceleration, any characteristics of posture or relaxation that are incorrect should be felt by the runner.

B. RELAXATION STRIDING—Practice striding with an exaggerated loose jaw and hands.

C. TIME COMPARISON—Compare the times of an acceleration run or sprint while practicing relaxation techniques versus that while "fighting" to increase speed.

D. MIND TRAINING—Have one or two additional athletes verbally harass the runner while he is practicing relaxation techniques to see if he can keep his mind on the task being performed.

Relaxation techniques can be a supplement to any program. They can be used during any phase of training and are especially effective for beginning runners and those athletes who are experiencing problems in the mechanics of running.

Flexibility Training

This program can be used before practice, after practice, or both. If used prior to a workout, a WARM-UP JOG of 440 to 880 yards should precede the exercises. The Flexibility Training can be taken every day during all phases of training and in all off season programs.

THE PROGRAM

1. Do not force or stretch any area by *bouncing*. This can lead to injury. The stretching must be done gradually and increased as flexibility develops.
2. Each exercise is to be performed 5 times. On the 5th repetition hold the stretch in a static position for 5 seconds at the full range of motion approaching the pain threshold for that specific area. RELEASE AND REPEAT. If the exercise is one sided, perform the movement twice for each side or part of the body. This will apply to Exercises #3, 6, 7, 9, 12, 13, and 16.

3. The format for each exercise is:
   A. Name of exercise.
   B. Areas of flexibility.
   C. Starting position for exercise.
   D. Movement of exercise.

THE EXERCISES

1. A. Warm-up. (Illustration 12-1)
   B. Upper body.
   C. Standing position, feet apart.
   D. ROTATE neck, fingers, wrists, arms, shoulders, and upper torso in all directions. FLEX and EXTEND the same parts (omit 5-second static stretch).

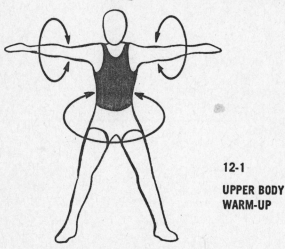

12-1

**UPPER BODY
WARM-UP**

2. A. Warm-up. (Illustration 12-2)
   B. Lower body.
   C. Seated in "L" position. Arms extended to side or supporting body.
   D. ROTATE toes, feet, ankles, knees, hips in all directions. FLEX and EXTEND the same parts. Lie on back for hip rotation (omit 5-second static stretch).

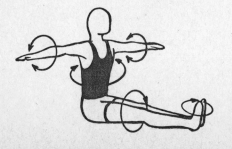

12-2

**LOWER BODY
WARM-UP**

3. A. Alternate leg crossover. (Illustration 12-3)
    B. Hamstring, groin, hip.
    C. Lying flat on back, legs together, arms extended, palms down.
    D. Lift leg straight over and touch opposite hand. Keep other leg, arm, hand, and back stationary.

12-3

**ALTERNATE LEG
CROSSOVER**

4. A. Overhead leg lift. (Illustration 12-4)
    B. Hip, abdomen, shoulders.
    C. Lying flat on back, legs together, arms straight at the sides.
    D. Lift legs over head and touch to ground. Keep the legs together and straight. Bend at the hips, keeping the upper body stationary. Return legs slowly to ground.

12-4

**OVERHEAD
LEG LIFT**

5. A. Overhead straddle leg lift. (Illustration 12-5)
    B. Hip, abdomen, groin, shoulders.
    C. Lying flat on back, legs spread wide apart, arms straight at the sides.
    D. Lift legs over head and touch to ground in straddle position. Keep the legs straight, bend at the hips, keeping the upper body stationary. Return legs slowly to the ground in straddle position.

12-5

OVERHEAD STRADDLE LEG LIFT

6. A. Hurdler's exercise. (Illustration 12-6)
    B. Hamstrings, quadriceps, groin.
    C. Seated position with one leg extended and the other leg tucked behind with the knee touching the ground.
    D. Bend forward with outstretched arms and touch the face below the knee area. Roll back slowly to a supine position. Keep the outstretched leg and the opposite knee flat on the ground.

12-6

HURDLER'S EXERCISE (TWO POSITIONS)

7. A. Straddle exercise. (Illustration 12-7)
    B. Hamstring, groin, shoulder.
    C. Seated position with legs as wide apart as possible.
    D. Bend forward with arms outstretched and touch the face
        below the knee area. Keep both legs straight and in contact
        with the ground.

12-7

STRADDLE EXERCISE

8. A. Forward stretch. (Illustration 12-8)
    B. Hamstring, groin, lower back.
    C. Seated position with legs as wide apart as possible, arms
        extended to the sides.
    D. Lower the upper body slowly towards the ground, keeping
        the legs straight and in contact with the ground.

12-8

FORWARD STRETCH

9. A. Quadriceps pull. (Illustration 12-9)
    B. Quadriceps.
    C. Standing position with or without support.
    D. Reach back and grab the opposite foot. Pull towards the
        buttocks in a lifting motion.

12-9

QUADRICEPS PULL

10. A. Backward stretch. (Illustration 12-10)
    B. Quadriceps, back.
    C. Kneeling position with legs slightly apart.
    D. Roll back slowly to the ground, keeping the knees in place. The hands can assist in maintaining balance.

12-10

BACKWARD STRETCH

11. A. Bend and reach. (Illustration 12-11)
    B. Hamstring, lower back, shoulder, abdomen.
    C. Seated position with legs together.
    D. Bend forward with arms outstretched and touch the face below the knee area. Keep both legs straight and in contact with the ground.

12-11

BEND AND REACH

12. A. Seated hamstring stretch. (Illustration 12-12)
    B. Hamstring.
    C. Seated position with legs extended.
    D. Lift leg up to side of head, keeping the knee straight and the extended leg flat on the ground.

12-12

SEATED
HAMSTRING STRETCH

13. A. Supine hamstring stretch. (Illustration 12-13)
     B. Hamstring.
     C. Lying flat on back with legs extended.
     D. Lift leg up to side of head, keeping the knee straight and the extended leg flat on the ground.

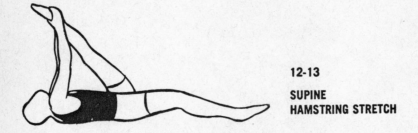

12-13

**SUPINE
HAMSTRING STRETCH**

14. A. Supported leg raise. (Illustration 12-14)
     B. Shoulder, abdomen.
     C. Seated position with legs extended. The arms and shoulders are extended behind the back as far as possible. Keep the head forward, chin towards chest.
     D. Lift legs to the head, keeping them straight. Return slowly to the ground.

12-14

SUPPORTED LEG RAISE

15. A. Groin stretch. (Illustration 12-15)
    B. Groin.
    C. Seated position with legs tucked, feet touching on the bottom.
    D. Lower knees to ground using one leg at a time, then both legs. The hands or elbows may press on the inside of the knees to add to the stretch.

12-15

GROIN STRETCH

16. A. Alternate leg stretch. (Illustration 12-16)
    B. Hamstring, groin.
    C. Standing position, feet wide apart.
    D. Bend forward with outstretched arms and touch the face below the knee area. Keep both legs straight.

12-16

**ALTERNATE
LEG STRETCH**

17. A. Hamstring stretch. (Illustration 12-17)
     B. Hamstring, lower back.
     C. Standing position with legs together.
     D. Bend forward with outstretched arms and touch the face
         below the knee area. Keep both legs straight.

12-17

HAMSTRING STRETCH

18. A. Front split. (Illustration 12-18)
     B. Hamstring, groin.
     C. Standing position with legs apart, one forward and one
         back.
     D. Slowly lower until the buttocks and groin touch the
         ground. Use hands for balance and support.

12-18

FRONT SPLIT

19. A. Side split. (Illustration 12-19)
    B. Groin, hamstring, hip, lower leg extension.
    C. Standing position, feet spread apart, toes pointed forward.
    D. Slowly lower until the crotch is as close to the ground as possible. Use hands for balance and support.

12-19

SIDE SPLIT

20. A. Heel cord stretch. (Illustration 12-20)
    B. Achilles tendon, lower leg extension.
    C. Stand at arm's distance from a wall, body inclined forward, back straight, feet flat, with hands at shoulder height and width from the wall.
    D. Bend forward until chest nearly touches the wall. Keep body straight and heels on floor. Progress by moving further away from the wall.

12-20

HEEL CORD STRETCH

21. A. Upper body lift. (Illustration 12-21)
     B. Upper back and trunk.
     C. Prone position on ground with arms clasped behind the head. A partner will support the lower legs and knees to keep them stationary.
     D. Slowly raise the upper torso as high as possible, keeping the head up. The abdominal area should be off the ground.

12-21

UPPER BODY LIFT

22. A. Bridge up. (Illustration 12-22)
     B. Quadricep, shoulder, lower back.
     C. Lying flat on back, place the hands behind the shoulders, and tuck the legs.
     D. Push up, arch the back, tilt the head back, and go up on the toes.

12-22

BRIDGE UP

23. A. Lower body lift. (Illustration 12-23)
     B. Lower back, hip, quadricep.
     C. Prone position on ground with arms folded under chin. A partner will apply pressure to the shoulder blades to keep the upper body stationary.
     D. Slowly lift the lower body as high as possible. Keep the legs straight and together and the thighs and hips off the ground.

12-23

LOWER BODY LIFT

24. A. Body arch. (Illustration 12-24)
     B. Back, shoulder, quadricep.
     C. Prone position on ground.
     D. Grasp ankles with hands. Pull on the legs and lift the upper body. Keep the head up and the thighs, hips, and chest off the ground.

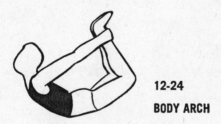

12-24

BODY ARCH

25. A. Suspended hanging. (Illustration 12-25)
     B. Overall body flexion and extension.
     C. Hang from a suspended bar, palms forward, hands at shoulder width and the feet about 12 inches off the ground.
     D. Hang relaxed for 5 seconds; now flex all of the body parts possible for 5 seconds; now extend all of the body parts possible for 5 seconds; hang relaxed for 5 seconds. Repeat once. The hanging periods should be extended to 10 seconds as flexibility improves.

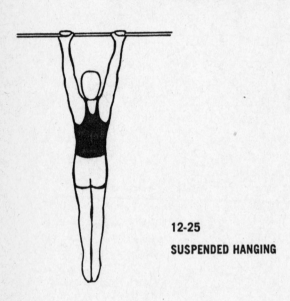

12-25

SUSPENDED HANGING

FLEXIBILITY TEST FOR RUNNERS

A. Sit and Reach Test.
B. Measures the flexion of the hip and back and the flexibility of the hamstring muscles.
C. Assume a sitting position with the legs extended about 12 inches apart at right angles to a line drawn on the floor. The heels should touch the near edge of the line. A partner may brace the feet so that upon reaching, the heels will not slip over the line.
D. The athlete should bend forward slowly three times without touching, then REACH with both hands as far forward as possible. TOUCH and HOLD. Take the best of 3 trials.
EQUIPMENT—A yardstick is taped between the legs of the athlete with the 15 inch mark on the heel line.
SCORING—The score is the number of inches reached on the yardstick.

ANALYSIS—The test is to be given every two weeks or approximately 10 workouts. A comparison of test scores will indicate whether or not flexibility is being improved and to what degree. A pretest should be given before the flexibility program is begun.

HOW TO SELECT AND PLAN PROGRAMS FOR IMPROVING SPEED

The selection and planning of programs for improving speed can be compared to the way a physician prescribes medication. It must suit the need of the patient as well as provide the proper treatment. It is necessary to know the individual for whom the program is intended. This knowledge is based on his physical and running ability as demonstrated by his present speed, strength, flexibility, running posture, and physical endurance. The type of speed needed, that is whether it is for a long or middle-distance runner or a sprinter, must also be considered. A simple four step procedure can be used for selection and planning: (A) *Observe*, (B) *Analyze*, (C) *Prescribe*, (D) *Follow Up*.

Observe

Watch the athlete RUN. Observe his start, acceleration, sprint, deceleration, and sustained running effort. The use of films from training sessions or competition are most beneficial. If possible, films should be taken from three angles: A front view, a rear view, and a side view of each athlete. An acceleration run of about 100 yards should serve the purpose and would use only 45 seconds of film per runner. Films can be used later for comparison to check improvement. Video taping if available is probably a less expensive method and would serve the same purpose.

Analyze

From observing the runner, determine what are his weaknesses, strengths, and needs. In what way can he improve upon his speed? Table 12-2 illustrates a form for use during observation. It can be used for films, video tape, or live sessions.

Prescribe

Based upon the analysis of the observations, a program for improving speed should be prescribed for the athlete if needed. It can be inte-

TABLE 12-2
OBSERVATION FORM FOR RUNNING SPEED

NAME_____ EVENTS_____
HGT._____ 440 YD. SPEED_____
WGT._____ 100 YD. SPEED_____
AGE_____ 50 YD. SPEED_____

		RATING				
	POOR	FAIR	AVER-AGE	GOOD	EXCEL-LENT	COM-MENTS
1. Stride Length	1	2	3	4	5	_____
2. Rate of Leg Movement	1	2	3	4	5	_____
3. Leg Strength & Power	1	2	3	4	5	_____
4. Body Strength & Power	1	2	3	4	5	_____
5. Flexibility	1	2	3	4	5	_____
6. Physical Endurance	1	2	3	4	5	_____
7. Relaxation While Running	1	2	3	4	5	_____
8. Running Posture	1	2	3	4	5	_____
9. Reaction Time (Sprinters Only)	1	2	3	4	5	_____
10. Overall Rating of Running Speed	1	2	3	4	5	_____

General Comments_____
_____
Analysis_____
_____
Recommendations_____
_____
Date_____Coach_____

grated as part of the regular training, serve as a supplement to regular training, or be used as developmental work in the off-season. Table 12-3 compares the areas for speed improvement, the programs described in this chapter and how they can affect the development of speed.

Follow Up

It should not be taken for granted that any speed program will work by itself. It is a combination of the athlete's intensity and desire to improve and the interest and input from the coach. Some basic guidelines to follow once a program has been prescribed are:

A. *Teach* the program to the athletes.
B. Be sure that they understand and can perform it correctly.
C. Set up the basic planning for them: how often the program should be used, when and where it should be used, how many repetitions, the rate of progression, etc.
D. Let the athlete know what to expect from the training and what results to look for. This will aid in the psychological approach to speed improvement as well as developing awareness.
E. Observe the program(s) in action whenever possible. Make any corrections and modifications necessary.
F. Be *patient* in expecting results. Evaluate the athlete and his progress periodically.

As stated previously, running speed can be improved by a variety of different methods although the degree of improvement cannot be determined ahead of time. Specific training programs for running speed are necessary for an athlete to work towards maximum potential. Since there are numerous ways in which speed is improved, it is not possible to select one program for all. In many instances, a combination of specialized programs may be needed.

TABLE 12-3
AREAS OF SPEED IMPROVEMENT AND THEIR DEVELOPMENT

PROGRAMS	STRIDE LENGTH	RATE OF LEG MOVEMENT	STRENGTH-POWER (LEGS AND BODY)	FLEXIBILITY	REACTION TIME	RUNNING POSTURE	PHYSICAL ENDURANCE
PUMP AND STRIDE	X	X					
DOWNHILL RUNNING	X	X				X	
UPHILL RUNNING		X	X				X
ACCELERATION RUNNING	X	X	X			X	X
TARGET TIME SPRINTING			X		X	X	X
FLEXIBILITY TRAINING	X			X			
STRENGTH TRAINING	X	X	X	X	X		
RELAXATION TECHNIQUES						X	

Index